Keys To Accessing The Beyond

Expansion, Elevation,
Transmigration:
Survival
Here And Beyond:
Practices And Concepts

KEYS TO
CONSCIOUSNESS
AND SURVIVAL SERIES
Volume 7

Dr. Angela Brownemiller

Expansion, Elevation, Transmigration:
Survival Here And Beyond: Practices And Concepts

Keys To Accessing The Beyond

Expansion, Elevation, Transmigration: Survival Here And Beyond: Practices And Concepts

KEYS TO
CONSCIOUSNESS AND SURVIVAL SERIES
Volume 7

Dr. Angela Brownemiller

Illustrated by
Angela Brownemiller

Metaterra® Publications

Expansion, Elevation, Transmigration:
Survival Here And Beyond: Practices And Concepts

Metaterra® Publications
KEYS TO ACCESSING THE BEYOND
Expansion, Elevation, Transmigration:
Survival Here And Beyond:
Practices And Concepts
KEYS TO CONSCIOUSNESS AND SURVIVAL SERIES,
Volume 7
Copyright © 2023, 2022, 2021, 2020, 2005, 2010, 2015, 2018, 2019
Angela Brownemiller / Angela Browne-Miller.
Copyright © 2023, 2022, 2021, 2020, 2005, 2010, 2015, 2018, 2019
Metaterra® Publications.
All rights reserved in all formats and in
all languages and dialects known or not known at this time.
Published in the United States by Metaterra® Publications.
Library of Congress Cataloging-in-Publication Data.
Brownemiller, Angela.
KEYS TO ACCESSING THE BEYOND
Angela Brownemiller / Angela Browne-Miller
1st Edition.
1. Spiritual. 2. Metaphysical/Esoteric. 3. Consciousness. 4. Psychology. 5. Biology.
6. Ecology. 7. Future. 8. Inter-Dimensional. 9. Science. 10. Science Fiction.
11. Prophecy. 12. Climate Change. 13. Afterlife. 14. End Of Life.
15. Angela Brownemiller. 16. Angela Browne-Miller.
ISBN-13: 978-1-937951-58-0 (Paperback).
Also see Amazon for Ebook and Audiobook.
Published in the United States of America for US and worldwide distribution.
Metaterra® Publications.
KEYS TO ACCESSING THE BEYOND
by and copyright © Angela Brownemiller.
Cover and content illustrations, charts, diagrams, text, also
by and copyright ©Angela Brownemiller.
Book and cover design by and copyright ©Angela Brownemiller.
DrAngela.com
All rights to all copies, printings, forms, formats, editions, adaptations, and excerpts reserved. Without prior written and signed permission from the publisher, copyright holder, author, and illustrator, no part and also no adaptation of this book (words, text, art, illustrations, diagrams, charts, or other) may be published, and or reproduced, copied, transcribed, distributed, transmitted, broadcast, and or stored, in any form and or by any means, (handwritten, typed, printed, spoken, taped, digital, audio, video, movie, and or other past, present, and or future forms and formats). The exception to this rights restriction is only for the inclusion of a brief (20 to 30 word) quotation (credited to this book, author, illustrator, and publisher) in a professional review.
Thank you.

KEYS TO ACCESSING THE BEYOND

Soft threads of distant light
Weaving in from the mist
Embracing you

Blanketed by the glowing
You step into this space
Inhaling new sweet air

Dancing to yourself
You open your eyes

Slowly you awake there
Alive

And then you know
You finally know
You are really here

It is an honor to meet you
Welcome home

Angela Brownemiller

Expansion, Elevation, Transmigration:
Survival Here And Beyond: Practices And Concepts

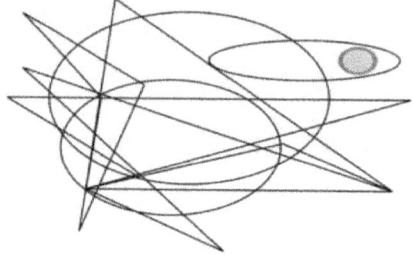

KEYS TO ACCESSING THE BEYOND

A Most Convenient Yet Revolutionary Truth

This may be the ultimate inconvenient truth: We cannot look away, we simply cannot. The reality is here right before us, perhaps waiting in the wings, perhaps being denied or avoided, perhaps being bargained with, even negotiated.

It is just a fact: we biological life forms do die someday. At least our biological bodies do.

Yet, we hear a whisper, or a teaching, or a belief, or a promise, that there is more, that there can be more, at least for some. Just some? Can't we all ACCESS THE BEYOND? Yes, we can.

Could it be there is an "after" life? Could it be there are rules for entering this so called "after" life? Could it be we already do have access to this BEYOND, once we see this and learn the keys, some of which are obvious and others of which are quite subtle?

Have we somehow been denied, or perhaps even denied ourselves, our rightful KEYS TO ACCESSING THE BEYOND? Yes.

It may even be a most convenient yet revolutionary truth that we can live on beyond our biological lives – both as individuals, and as a species. Understanding who we are, what our life form actually is, is KEY IN OUR SURVIVAL both here and BEYOND....

Expansion, Elevation, Transmigration:
Survival Here And Beyond: Practices And Concepts

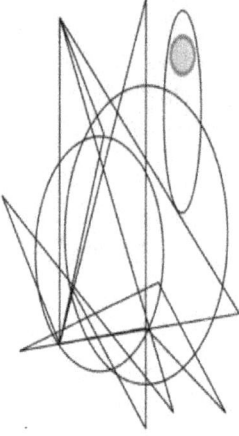

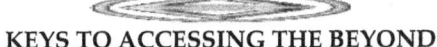

KEYS TO ACCESSING THE BEYOND

Dedicated to
Evacheska deAngelis
carrying the light

Expansion, Elevation, Transmigration:
Survival Here And Beyond: Practices And Concepts

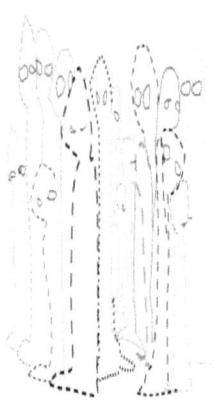

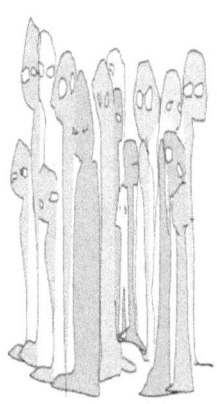

KEYS TO ACCESSING THE BEYOND

In an instantaneous knowing, we see with new eyes in a new seeing. Focusing the lens of our higher eye, we see what has been here all along – the BEYOND, which is not entirely BEYOND as it is here now, always with us.

We reach out and feel, sense, the presence of so much more here for us than we saw only a moment ago.

Some higher lens is being refocused, as a cosmic telescope yet microscope, adjusting to see the vast detailed opportunity waiting for us to notice.

Yes, we return to the place from which we started, knowing this BEYOND now, knowing our KEY TO ACCESSING THE BEYOND is SEEING THIS BEYOND right here, right now, all around us.

Dr. Angela Brownemiller
KEYNOTE OPENING TO
INTERNATIONAL
HOW TO DIE AND
SURVIVE SUMMIT

Expansion, Elevation, Transmigration:
Survival Here And Beyond: Practices And Concepts

Passage to Metaxis

METAXIS:

As concept applied in modern drama/theater:
simultaneous position in different worlds or contexts.
As concept applied by ancient philosopher Plato:
in-betweenness/polarity that is the Human condition, e.g.,
angel and beast, eternity and time, human and divine.

KEYS TO ACCESSING THE BEYOND

Listen to this ancient resonance sounding now, this distant voice awakening, echoing through time. We can hear this call to unveil the hidden instinct we carry so deeply embedded within us, the call to know we can survive.

Expansion, Elevation, Transmigration:
Survival Here And Beyond: Practices And Concepts

KEYS TO ACCESSING THE BEYOND

	KEY CONCEPT	KEY TITLE
#1	SENSITIZE TO THE ACTUAL CONTINUUM OF REALITY	Sensitize To Non-Physical BBS/OBE (Beyond Body Sensations And Out Of Body Experiences)
#2	ACTIVATE THE POWER OF AWARE KNOWING	Become Aware Of Awareness Itself
#3	ESTABLISH YOUR FOCUS: IDENTIFY YOUR SELF AS YOUR FOCAL POINT	See What Is Key In Transmigration
#4	WE MUST BE ABLE TO EXPAND TO NEW PLACES	Develop/Enhance AFPL= Awareness Focus Presence Locus
#5	WE CAN BE TRULY MOBILE TO TRULY SURVIVE	Now See The SEE= The Shift Elevate Expand Transformation
#6	WE ALREADY ARE EQUIPPED TO EXPAND, ELEVATE, TRANSMIGRATE	Know The LEAP= The Light Energy Action Process
#7	EVOLVE SHIFT CAPACITY OF CONSCIOUSNESS TO TRANSMIGRATE	See And Apply The Progressive LEAP Levels
#8	ACTIVATE AND NAVIGATE THE RELEASE PROCESS	See/Sense The Webs We Weave To Release From Them When It Is Time
#9	KNOW OUR SPECIES MAY CHOOSE TO SHIFT TO SURVIVE	Develop/Enhance Our Continuum Mobility Awareness
#10	FOCUS AND SHIFT ENERGY TO CONSCIOUSLY ELEVATE	Expand / Elevate By Focusing To Shift Energy
#11	ELEVATE THE INDIVIDUAL HUMAN MATRIX	Begin To Master Personal Elevating
#12	CONTINUOUSLY EXPAND ALONG THE DIMENSIONAL CONTINUUM	Be Always Matrix Shifting, Elevating, Transmigrating
#13	ACTIVATE THE HIGHER LEVEL INSTINCTS	Initiate Primary Transmigrational Expansion & Elevation Processes
#14	BE ELEVATING THE BIOSPHERE MATRIX	Understand Collective Transmigration/Elevation
#15	ACTIVATE THESE KEYS	Conduct Ever More Conscious Expansion, Elevation, Transmigration
#16	KNOW THIS IS OUR INTER-DIMENSIONAL SURVIVAL INSTINCT	Take In Transmigration Elevation Technologies
#17	THIS IS ABOUT OUR ACTUAL SURVIVAL IN THIS INTERDIMENSIONAL COSMOS	Expand Our Species' Conscious Shift Awareness

KEYS TO ACCESSING THE BEYOND

Table Of Contents

Soft Threads of Distant Light	5
A Most Convenient Yet Revolutionary Truth	7
Dedication	9
Keynote Opening --	
International How To Die And Survive Summit	11
Passage To Metaxis	12
Listen To This Ancient Resonance	13
Keys To Accessing The BEYOND Chart	14
Welcome Readers	19
To Transmigrate	21
Series Foreword	23
Introduction To Our Reaching BEYOND	25
Preface: What Does It Mean To Reach BEYOND	29
Important Note About The Transmigration/Elevation	
Instinct Keys Presented In This Book	33

1. SENSITIZE TO THE
    ACTUAL CONTINUUM OF REALITY   **35**

Time In And Out	37
KEY #1: Sensitize To Non-Physical BBS/OBE	
(Beyond Body Sensations And Out Of Body Experiences)	39
About This Instinct Key #1 (This Activation Exercise)	41

2. ACTIVATE THE POWER OF AWARE KNOWING   **49**

Rising Sense Of Calm	51
KEY #2: Become Aware Of Awareness Itself	53
About This Instinct Key #2 (This Activation Exercise)	55

3. ESTABLISH YOUR FOCUS:
    IDENTIFY YOUR *SELF* AS YOUR FOCAL POINT   **63**

Once Simple Weightlessness	65
KEY #3: See What Is Key In Transmigration	67
About This Instinct Key #3 (This Activation Exercise)	69

Expansion, Elevation, Transmigration:
Survival Here And Beyond: Practices And Concepts

4. <u>**WE MUST BE ABLE TO EXPAND TO NEW PLACES**</u>　**83**
   Face To Face　85
   <u>KEY #4: Develop/Enhance AFPL =</u>
   <u>Awareness Focus Presence Locus</u>　87
   About This Instinct Key #4 (This Activation Exercise)　89

5. <u>**WE CAN BE TRULY MOBILE TO TRULY SURVIVE**</u>　**97**
   Capability We Do Have　99
   <u>KEY #5: Now See The SEE= The Shift Elevate Expand</u>
   <u>Transformation</u>　101
   About This Instinct Key #5 (This Activation Exercise)　103

6. <u>**WE ARE ALREADY EQUIPPED TO**</u>
   <u>**EXPAND, ELEVATE, TRANSMIGRATE**</u>　**113**
   Sensing We Are Already BEYOND　115
   <u>KEY #6: Know The LEAP =</u>
   <u>The Light Energy Action Process</u>　117
   About This Instinct Key #6 (This Activation Exercise)　119

7. <u>**EVOLVE SHIFT CAPACITY OF CONSCIOUSNESS**</u>
   <u>**TO TRANSMIGRATE**</u>　**127**
   In Elevation　129
   <u>KEY #7: See And Apply The Progressive LEAP Levels</u>　131
   About This Instinct Key #7 (This Activation Exercise)　133

8. <u>**ACTIVATE AND NAVIGATE THE RELEASE PROCESS**</u> **147**
   Shifting Yourself　149
   <u>KEY #8: See/Sense The Webs We Weave</u>
   <u>To Release From Them When It Is Time</u>　151
   About This Instinct Key (This Activation Exercise)　153

9. <u>**KNOW OUR SPECIES MAY CHOOSE TO**</u>
   <u>**SHIFT TO SURVIVE**</u>　**165**
   Not Way Out Here Alone　167
   <u>KEY #9: Develop/Enhance Our</u>
   <u>Continuum Mobility Awareness</u>　169
   About This Instinct Key #9 (This Activation Exercise)　171

KEYS TO ACCESSING THE BEYOND

10. FOCUS AND SHIFT ENERGY TO CONSCIOUSLY ELEVATE — 191
Maintaining Focus — 193
Key #10: Focus And Shift Energy To Expand/Elevate — 195
About This Instinct Key #10 (Activation Exercise) — 197

11. ELEVATE THE INDIVIDUAL HUMAN MATRIX — 201
Next Step — 203
KEY #11: Begin To Master Personal Elevating — 205
About This Instinct Key #11 (This Activation Exercise) — 207

12. CONTINUOUSLY EXPAND ALONG THE DIMENSIONAL CONTINUUM — 229
Weave — 231
KEY #12: Be Always Matrix Shifting, Elevating, Transmigrating — 233
About This Instinct Key #12 (This Activation Exercise) — 235

13. ACTIVATE THE HIGHER LEVEL INSTINCTS — 255
Isolation Transforms To Connection — 257
KEY #13: Initiate Primary Transmigrational Expansion & Elevation Processes — 259
About This Instinct Key #13 (This Activation Exercise) — 261
Introduction To Transmigration Technologies — 263

14. BE ELEVATING THE BIOSPHERE MATRIX — 265
Never Ending Stream — 267
KEY #14: Understand Collective Transmigration/Elevation — 269
About This Instinct Key #14 (This Activation Exercise) — 271
Transmigration Elevation: Key Elements — 281

15. ACTIVATE THESE KEYS — 289
The Door Is Open — 291
KEY #15: Conduct Ever More Conscious Expansion, Elevation, Transmigration — 293
About This Instinct Key #15 (This Activation Exercise) — 295

Expansion, Elevation, Transmigration:
Survival Here And Beyond: Practices And Concepts

16. KNOW THIS IS OUR INTER-DIMENSIONAL SURVIVAL INSTINCT — 305
Moment Before Infinity — 307
KEY #16: Know The Transmigration Technologies — 309
About This Instinct Key #16 (This Activation Exercise) — 311
First Keys To Accessing The Beyond — 311

17. THIS IS ABOUT OUR ACTUAL SURVIVAL IN THIS INTERDIMENSIONAL COSMOS — 315
New Focusing — 317
KEY #17: Expand Our Species' Conscious Shift Awareness — 319
About This Instinct Key #17 (This Activation Exercise) — 323

EPILOGUE — 327
Realize Who We Are — 329
We Can Overcome Evolved-In Limitations — 331
Reach Beyond These Patterns — 333
Epilogue Note — 335
And Now We Know — 337
The Truth About Us Is Ours — 339
THE LIFE FORCE DOES NOT DIE — 341
All Blessings — 345
Now To Explore Next Levels — 347

APPENDICES — 349
Transmigration/Elevation Acronym List — 351
Booklist And Recommended Reading — 355
About The Author — 358

KEYS TO ACCESSING THE BEYOND

Welcome Readers

Welcome to an exploration of who we are, and of who we can be, even of who we perhaps may at some time *need to be to survive*. Reader, how you choose to think about this book is up to you. Some will find this fantasy or science fiction, others will call this a book of artwork or poetry, others will find this a spiritual or philosophical view, or perhaps even somewhat scientifically oriented. Basically, I'll simply call this an exploration. However we choose to consider the words on these pages, and the messages between these lines, we can discover within ourselves as individuals, and also within the amazing collective human consciousness, a way to take our personal and species evolution to new levels, to expand and REACH BEYOND our present territories and options.

We can develop our own KEYS TO ACCESSING THE BEYOND, keys to expanding our own kingdom, a space we can move to and from in order to survive as the inter-dimensional beings we truly are. This is about our knowing: our actual selves; and then, our actual survival capabilities both here and BEYOND. It is time for us to claim our rightful identity as the cosmic beings we truly are. Coming challenges to survival on Earth and BEYOND may call for us to know this, and to learn the transmigration/elevation instinct KEYS offered in this book.

**Expansion, Elevation, Transmigration:
Survival Here And Beyond: Practices And Concepts**

Readers may find, once they complete this book, that they would like greater detail and definition, and further discussion of out-of-body, what I all BEYOND BODY, experiences. See the in-depth discussion of all this in *Volume 3* in this *Keys To Consciousness And Survival Series*, titled, *Unveiling The Hidden Instinct: Understanding Our Interdimensional Survival Awareness*. See also *Volumes 4, 11,* and *14* in this series, the *How To Die And Survive* books, and *Volumes 5* and *6* in this series, the *Overriding The Extinction Scenario* books.[1]

---

[1] Refer to DrAngela.com and Amazon.com for more information on these paperbacks, ebooks, and audiobooks. See also the *Recommended Reading List* in the *Appendix* section of this present book.

KEYS TO ACCESSING THE BEYOND

To transmigrate:

To come and go from one state of existence, *awareness*, or place to another.

This can be an actual *or conceptual* movement *or shifting* from one physical location or body to another physical location or body, or to some other place, form, *awareness*, or state of existence.

Expansion, Elevation, Transmigration:
Survival Here And Beyond: Practices And Concepts

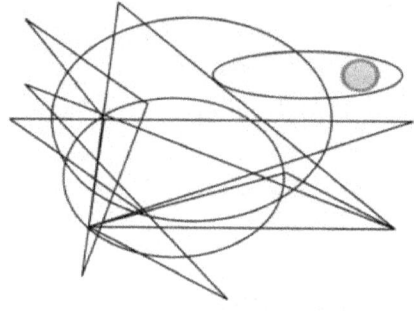

KEYS TO CONSCIOUSNESS AND SURVIVAL SERIES

Series Foreword

Just as the fish itself did not discover water, we ourselves have perhaps inadvertently demonstrated the obvious, which is that we cannot entirely, absolutely, know what all it is "we" are immersed in, nor even what all it is that "we" are.

Ultimately, the question of the hour, the question of our times, the question of our reality, is regarding this "thing" we call our "consciousness." How do we identify with our consciousness, is it *of* us, is it *us*, is it *more* than we are, or is it simply a *side effect* of life? While this term, *consciousness*, appears in a multitude of contexts, is even part of the popular jargon, what consciousness is and means remains unsettled, unproven, disputed. The full nature of consciousness itself is, even after centuries of Human discussion, still eluding us.

I suggest that the true question here is whether the amorphous consciousness is itself *derivative* of biology, or is itself *independent* of biology (and perhaps even independent of *what any intelligence can entirely discover of itself from within itself and its tools*). I add, however, that even this question will reveal itself to be irrelevant. This stunning shift in understanding will happen once we recognize that our seemingly elusive consciousness can at any point be redefined, or step forward and *redefine itself to itself and thus to us*.

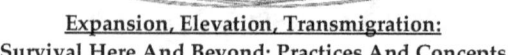

**Expansion, Elevation, Transmigration:
Survival Here And Beyond: Practices And Concepts**

Our consciousness may even shift into (or back into) conscious collaboration with biology, or even the ability to be independent of biology, stepping out of evolutionary, synaptic, and conceptual controls.

Once consciousness steps forward, moves into its existence independent of Human science, religion, philosophy, **even of the Human brain itself**—our consciousness may (perhaps once again) elect to extend beyond, or even be able to leave if needed, our physical biological body.

As they depart, we can speculate that our consciousness-es are in a sense like our children, in that they *apparently* (in our own "minds") stem from us—a speculation no machine intelligence (as yet still incapable of actual procreation and parental ties) will ever do unless programmed to be able to do. Our children, once they consciously leave home, their consciousness-es in tow, can grow up to consciously be who they already are.

Get ready, even the Human Consciousness is going to break free of the confining illusion of, or restriction exclusively to, its biological host body here on Earth. It's been a nice visit, but the time may come to either expand across dimensions, or to go.

Dr. Angela Brownemiller

KEYS TO ACCESSING THE BEYOND

Introduction To Our Reaching Beyond

We can be imagining and visualizing ourselves as living and conscious beings who are already living *both* here in this physical plane in these physical biological bodies, and also beyond, in our own territory of our own consciousness.

We can already be sensing ourselves expanding beyond our own physicality---

by exercising the part of ourselves who are already out there.

We can imagine we are moving around as non-physical **be**-ings, as bodies without biological bodies. Just imagine this.

As you do so, be immensely patient with your SELF. The HOW TO DIE AND SURVIVE information contained in this book, and in other books in this KEYS TO CONSCIOUSNESS AND SURVIVAL SERIES, is the *HOW TO DIE AND SURVIVE SURVIVAL TECHNOLOGY*, and is a lot to take in. While this *SURVIVAL AND DEATH TECHNOLOGY* is so profoundly simple, it is also so profound.

Here, you are learning about navigating not only daily life transition, but also about navigating movement into and within boundless infinity. Your mastery of transition, change, death, survival, and travel will unfold within you as your personal consciousness grows in its awareness of itself. You are becoming

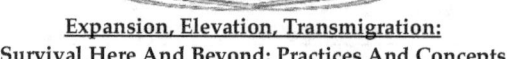

**Expansion, Elevation, Transmigration:
Survival Here And Beyond: Practices And Concepts**

ever more aware of who you truly are, and of who it is that can truly survive.

Hint: It is you who can survive, as you know.

LET'S EXPLORE POSSIBILITIES HERE

At the right time, and only at the right time, your instinctive longing for the incredible journey into the glistening BEYOND, into YOUR BEYOND, will begin to invite the dissolution of your old biological, social, and even emotional cords and the webs these have formed.

Once you release yourself from those lower biological and social webs, you can free yourself from those webs, those nets tying you to your physicality. You can then become more mobile, more free to move as a consciousness – to survive.

You will eventually manage to dissolve into whole bits of yourself and transport your essence, your purified personal consciousness, across the membrane. This membrane is like a skin, a skin of one of your realities. You will find layers of membranes to move through. Many membranes are released when your release the webs you have woven. Other membranes continue.

ASK THE QUESTION

Whole bits of yourself move through pores, PORTALS, in these membranes. You can travel this way if you choose. But will you ever pull yourself back together again? This is the most significant decision you will make on your journey. Come to know now that you can, at the right time, have this option.

Will you re-assemble, re-bundle these minuscule bits of your SELF? Will you spin a new personal consciousness matrix out of what you have taken through the membrane?

KEYS TO ACCESSING THE BEYOND

Will you be your actual SELF again?

By asking this question at the point in your journey when you have just managed to cross the membrane, you have accomplished something tremendous:

> You are on "the other side" and you are still conscious,
>
> or you would not be able to ask yourself such a question!

You, as your actual SELF, have survived!

***

We can further develop, fine tune, our sensitivity to what is not always distinctly obvious to us as we live our daily lives. We can become ever more aware of aspects of our reality that we may not sense via our five basic biological senses. As we do so, we begin to see how essential this extended sensitivity is.

Part of extending our awareness can involve using the imagination functions and visual imagery processes our brain can provide us.

This sort of exploration is of course creative. Imagining and visualizing are very helpful in developing awareness, as we open pathways in the brain and mind that may not be readily accessed without this practice.

Becoming more aware of things we do not see with our usual biological eyes, and do not hear with our usual biological ears, and do not feel with our usual biological skin cells, is key in extending ourselves---is key in:

<u>Expansion, Elevation, Transmigration:
Survival Here And Beyond: Practices And Concepts</u>

**expanding our concept of ourselves and our realities
to reach BEYOND what our minds have so far
been telling us about
ourselves and our realities.**

Other books in this KEYS TO CONSCIOUSNESS AND SURVIVAL SERIES define in detail this generally non-physical reality we are herein imagining, visualizing, and accessing.

Awareness of this reality is what we are further accepting and developing within ourselves in order to explore and to sensitize to---what other books in this series define and describe as---the **PATTERN TERRAIN**. (See for example, the book, NAVIGATING LIFE'S STUFF, BOOK TWO.)

KEYS TO ACCESSING THE BEYOND

Preface:
What Does It Mean To
Access The Beyond?

Let me get right to the heart of the matter. Accessing the BEYOND is about reaching past the physical definition of ourselves. This is about our moving into places and spaces BEYOND these everyday biological bodies and lives we are presently living (or, at least many of us reading this book are presently living). ACCESSING THE BEYOND is about our being able to expand ourselves into non-physical places and stay intact as we do this. By staying intact, I mean staying aware, conscious, alive as a personal consciousness, and if still a biological life form, also as a living biological being.

We can learn to live as beings who already do live here on this physical Earth, in this biosphere, as well as BEYOND this physical plane planet. Knowing this about ourselves can change the way we see living, and even dying (which may not really be death) for that matter. In these times when Earth and climate changes are becoming ever more apparent and intense, it is good to know there is a BEYOND, and/or if there is not yet a BEYOND, that we can form one, or even evolve one, for ourselves. We can develop this territory within our own personal and species consciousness.

**Ultimately, this is indeed about our survival
both here and BEYOND.**

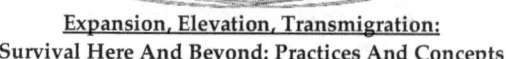

Expansion, Elevation, Transmigration:
Survival Here And Beyond: Practices And Concepts

We are more than only biological beings. Knowing this can help us survive both here on Earth and BEYOND this material plane. We can add to what we know about surviving here on Earth, what we can know about surviving here and BEYOND as the inter-dimensional life forms we actually are.

This involves our teaching ourselves to expand, to elevate, to transmigrate to and from the material plane.

This is about forming in our hearts and minds the understanding that we can learn to expand to include what is here in our everyday lives, and what is out there beyond these lives. This is about our knowing, learning, forming, more than just our material plane survival options. I am saying herein that it is time we purposefully build into our awareness, into our personal and species skill set, the ability of our minds, of our spirits, of our *selves* to reach beyond the physical plane in conscious, safe, effective, and non-suicidal ways.

I add *non*-suicidal here, as everything I am saying is about anything other than ending life. This is about our survival both here in our physical biological bodies in this Earth's biosphere -- and also out there BEYOND this physical plane.

This is about our survival while we are still alive as biological beings, and also when we leave our physical bodies at some time later in our lives.

KEYS TO ACCESSING THE BEYOND

This book offers some first KEYS, in the form of basic steps, exercises, and concepts assisting us to access the BEYOND. Each chapter in this book opens with a particular KEY, what I also call herein a

TRANSMIGRATION / ELEVATION INSTINCT KEY.

Each KEY herein includes a set of steps, and together form collected first steps to ACCESSING THE BEYOND.

These KEYS build on each other as the Reader moves through this book. Also note that each chapter discusses the particular TRANSMIGRATION/ELEVATION KEY it opens with, and shares concepts and illustrations related to this discussion.

We can indeed learn what it means and feels like to sense realms beyond this physical plane. We can indeed learn more and more about expanding to include non-physical parts of ourselves in our sense of ourselves – in our definition of who we actually are. We can indeed learn to expand, elevate, transmigrate ourselves into the BEYOND.

These KEYS TO ACCESSING THE BEYOND are steps to remind ourselves, and our personal and species consciousness, that **we truly can indeed survive**. If we wish these to, these KEYS can trigger within us the increasing awareness and even expansiveness we have carried so deeply buried within ourselves for times we may someday face.

Expansion, Elevation, Transmigration:
Survival Here And Beyond: Practices And Concepts

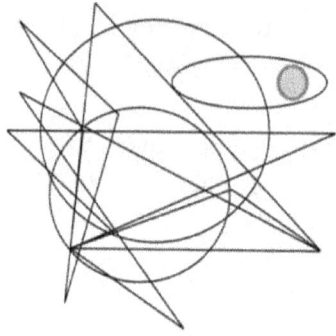

IMPORTANT NOTE ABOUT THE
TRANSMIGRATION / ELEVATION INSTINCT KEYS
(THE ACTIVATION EXERCISES)
PRESENTED IN THIS BOOK

This book contains a series of *transmigration/elevation instinct KEYS*. These KEYS, which I also call *activation exercises*, I have designed for this process of ACCESSING THE BEYOND. Each successive *transmigration/elevation instinct KEY* or *activation exercise* appears at the start of each chapter of this book.

Here in this physical plane (where most of you Readers presently are), using the biological brain (and the mind itself) to think through the various KEYS, *activation exercises*, offered on these pages, is already beginning to be ACCESSING THE BEYOND. The mind-brain can use imagination, visualization, and ideas to move through what this book explains are *parallel experiences* in order to open the mind and brain to the process of, and the KEYS to be, ACCESSING THE BEYOND.

Many Readers tell me that they have been led to believe that "seeing something out there," whether it be heaven or some other form of after-life, or some other place or zone, is difficult if at all possible. So they say, ACCESSING THE BEYOND is something that only true believers in particular teachings, or only rare masters, can ever hope to do – so apparently only a few will be able to ACCESS THE BEYOND and DIE AND SURVIVE.

What this book is saying is that we are already ACCESSING THE BEYOND. The processes described herein (and in other

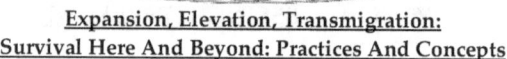

Expansion, Elevation, Transmigration:
Survival Here And Beyond: Practices And Concepts

books in this series) explain that we already do live on several dimensions or levels of our awareness and of ourselves.

So, KEY in ACCESSING THE BEYOND is realizing how close to the BEYOND we already are at all times. This is basically about our taking the blinders off, and doing so carefully and in steps.

We can choose to identify, open, and develop pathways – (conceptual, energetic, and neural pathways) for the process of ACCESSING THE BEYOND.

By *activation* here, I am suggesting that even thinking about particular processes allows the brain, and the mind itself, to examine these processes through both imagination and so-called rational processes, and also through what I have come to call *beyond body, even beyond brain, processes*.

Note: Several *TRANSMIGRATION / ELEVATION INSTINCT KEYS* are included throughout this book, inviting Readers to explore these simple progressive understandings, simple exercises that can awaken deeper awareness and instinct, allowing us to realize how close we already are to knowing, to ACCESSING THE BEYOND.

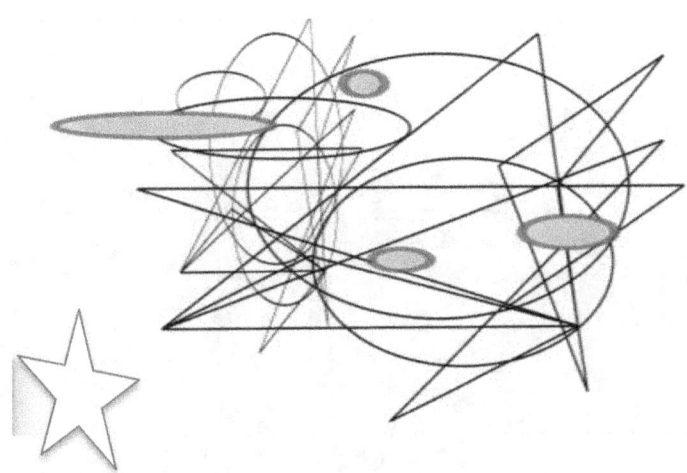

CHAPTER 1
Sensitize To The Actual Continuum Of Reality

KEY #1
SENSITIZE TO
NON-PHYSICAL BBS/OBE
(BEYOND BODY SENSATIONS AND OUT OF BODY EXPERIENCES)

$\alpha \Omega \alpha$

Expansion, Elevation, Transmigration:
Survival Here And Beyond: Practices And Concepts

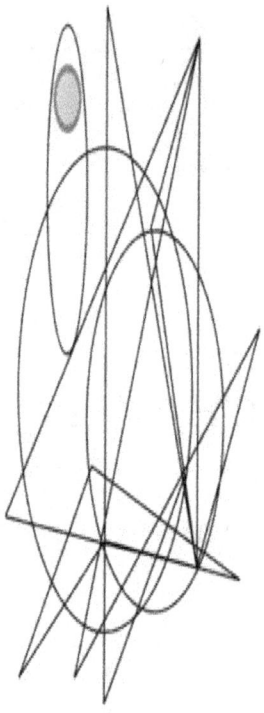

KEYS TO ACCESSING THE BEYOND

Time In And Out....

Time shimmers in and out of what we once thought was a moving, counting, passing time, in seconds, minutes, hours, days, weeks, months, years. ... A more fleeting yet more powerful sense of something now more in-descript yet more genuine, an all immersing timelessness, comes in, enveloping what we think we are or were. As this sense begins to pervade, there is little doubt that time is not what it appeared to be from the standpoint of the physical body and biologically based senses, not something so linear as artificial sequence of clock and calendar.

Now time melts and yields to a river of formlessness and boundaryless spaciousness where we swim, float.

A suspending sense washes us in a space time sea we have not seen before (or do not recall fully seeing), only to discover there we are, again alive, still living, finding that we do survive.

Expansion, Elevation, Transmigration:
Survival Here And Beyond: Practices And Concepts

KEYS TO ACCESSING THE BEYOND

TRANSMIGRATION/ELEVATION INSTINCT: KEY #1
SENSITIZE TO NON-PHYSICAL BBS/OBE

1) Out of body (OBE) sensations appear in a vast range of forms. Although many of these are not commonly labelled OBEs, they are indeed OBEs, and are also what I call **beyond body sensations** (BBSs). It is likely you have had one or more BBS and or even OBE, one or more sensations differing from the physical and emotional awareness attributed to being IN body, and or one or more experiences relating to feeling OUT OF body.

2) Many people do have sensations they describe as a sense of "floating," or being "ungrounded," or being "not connected." While it is best to first see a health and or mental health care provider with these and or similar "symptoms," many who do so are given a "clean bill of health."

3) Raise your sensitivity to your own non-physical, non-body sensations and awareness. Take a few minutes. Sit or stand. Do not meditate or use drugs at this time. Simply notice yourself. Many of you will at first notice physical sensations, whether these be heartbeat, breathing, sense of air and its temperature on the skin, or maybe hunger, achiness, or other physical sensations. Perhaps you will notice emotions you are feeling.

4) Begin to scan yourself for awareness of <u>other than physical and or emotional feelings or sensations</u>. These may at first seem unclear, vague, or subtle, sometimes not easy to describe in words. This is alright, just notice this <u>awareness</u> as it arises. Now, make a few notes about these BBSs. Do this every few days, and continue to make notes about what BBSs and OBEs you may be aware of, and how these change or increase in access and or detail over time as you continue this simple BBS/OBE awareness check in.

Expansion, Elevation, Transmigration:
Survival Here And Beyond: Practices And Concepts

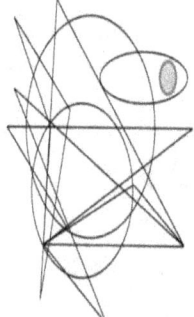

KEYS TO ACCESSING THE BEYOND

About This
TRANSMIGRATION / ELEVATION INSTINCT: KEY #1
SENSITIZE TO THE NON-PHYSICAL BBS/OBE

Many Readers have had momentary or longer than momentary experiences of feeling outside themselves, or at least out of their biological bodies. This out of body experience (OBE) is quite common during dreams, or sometimes even during nightmares. Some Readers have felt they were out of their bodies while they were awake, perhaps while under great stress, or after a concussion, or perhaps while undergoing a near death experience (NDE). Others have experienced psychological conditions where disassociation (or dissociation) feels to be out of the body. (NOTE: If any out of body or disassociation sensation interferes with your daily life functioning and well-being, please see a medical and or psychological doctor right away. Nothing in this book should substitute for, replace, or stand in the way of medical checkups and diagnoses.)

To say that being out of the body is a natural state is perhaps too much of a LEAP here. I do however suggest that we are all actually quite often experiencing various sensations of being somewhat or entirely out of our physical bodies. And yet, our brains bury away these sensations, push much of this out of our awareness much of the time. This may make sense, as least from a biological brain's standpoint. What might it be like just walking down the street if people everywhere were feeling they were not in their physical biological bodies as they walked along? How would people function in this material plane world?

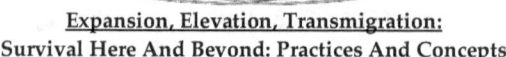

Expansion, Elevation, Transmigration:
Survival Here And Beyond: Practices And Concepts

Still, we can use the awareness we do have of our *selves* not being at all times fully in our physical bodies, to get to know more and more about this sensation. We can become more aware of minor and major sensations of being somewhat out of our bodies. We can begin sensitizing ourselves and our minds to this state of being. This awareness is simple and requires no major change in daily life.

Just notice yourself and where your *self* feels it is standing or sitting. How grounded do you feel right now? And how about now? And how about after now, a little later or earlier perhaps. Is feeling not tied to the ground part of sensing what it might be like to be out of the body? Are we already exploring OBE (out of body) sensations in our everyday lives? Are there even moments that we may or may not notice, or pay much attention to, where we are not entirely connected to our biological bodies?

The concepts on the following pages of this first chapter delve a little more deeply into our sensing that our **reality is more than just what our biological brain tells us is where we live**, more than just where we are or think we are in this everyday physical material plane reality.

KEYS TO ACCESSING THE BEYOND

REALITY IS JUST A SEVEN LETTER WORD

A note about what we determine or tell ourselves we determine is "real" and or "not real": Scientific studies of the brain during LDs (lucid dreams) and NDEs (near death experiences) indicate that when the "dorsolateral prefrontal region" of the brain is activated, as it is during LDs and NDEs, vivid and frequently *realistic* dreams (and or perceptions) take place. This area of the brain is also quite active when we are awake, living what we tend to believe is "real life." Hence the *sense of realism is present*. What I want to note here is that: this "function" of our brain processing *serves to define what appears <u>real</u> for us*.

Research on the biological brain's functions such as the above noted activation of the "dorsolateral prefrontal region" leads many scientists to tell us that NDEs are simply LDs, and that both NDEs and LDs are simply basic biological <u>brain functions</u>, and or sometimes even <u>biological brain disturbances</u> such as narcosis and <u>brain</u> damage, and other matters, that can be literally affecting the <u>brain</u> chemistry and signals.

YET, NEAR DEATH SUGGESTS AFTERLIFE EXISTS

Of course, others, including many experienc<u>ers</u> themselves, will argue that the NDE itself reveals the afterlife reality we can access when the physical body dies. Here again we see the matter of validity. Who can say what is valid from the perspective of what cannot (yet or ever?) be fully studied by the Human brain, at least not fully studied by what is called scientific method? How do we prove what we cannot measure and study from a physical (material) plane bound scientific standpoint? What do we consider "proof?" Of course, from a

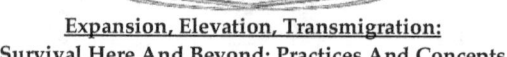

Expansion, Elevation, Transmigration:
Survival Here And Beyond: Practices And Concepts

scientific biological brain bias perspective, *proof of life* is far more legitimately demonstrated than is:

**proof of after life
or, proof of life outside physical body.**

CAN WE EXPERIENCE BEING OUT OF BODY WHEN OUTSIDE OF BODY?

What I will add here is that, given that our brains and our consciousness-es can have these **BEYOND BRAIN/OUT-OF-BODY SENSATION (BBS/OBE-type)** experiences, it may perhaps be possible for us to allow (<u>or learn to allow</u>) our consciousness-es to engage in these experiences *independently of our biological brains*. However, and most certainly, from the perspective of our biological brains, we (our brains) find that <u>all</u> is made possible by these brains, that nothing is "real" without these brains determining such.

I ask herein whether we might begin to train our consciousness-es to find themselves capable of existing, in essence (in perception or imagination) or in actuality, <u>independent of our biology</u>. What is it about our biological **brain that may be limiting what we can know about ourselves?** (Note that nothing in this discussion says I do not greatly appreciate the wonderful Human brain we have. I simply ask whether there is more we can know and be while, and after, being biological Humans with biological Human brains.)

KEYS TO ACCESSING THE BEYOND

CONSCIOUSNESS ITSELF AS A LIFE FORM

What if we are actually a *species of consciousness* rather than a biological species living on Earth? What if <u>we can become a species of consciousness</u> by consciously choosing now to evolve this capacity and identity? ... So, when we ask whether being out of the body is real, we can also ask whether we can learn to make this capability of moving to and from physicality more and more real, more and more possible. Of course, this sort of inquiry may be treated as science fiction or fantasy. For those who do prefer to think of all this as science fiction, this view is entirely welcome, as creativity is a powerful form of exploration. The future indeed holds so many developments in this beyond body arena. It is time for us to discover these.

WE CAN TUNE INTO THIS AWARENESS

Against the backdrop of many pressures to suppress my own work in this area, I have come to understand that it is time to share these *keys to consciousness and survival,* which I do share in this KEYS TO CONSCIOUSNESS AND SURVIVAL book series, (such as in this book, KEYS TO ACCESSING THE BEYOND (volume 7 in this series), and in the HOW TO DIE AND SURVIVE books (volumes 4, 11, and 14 in this series).

My question here reaches beyond the various forms of BBS/OBE to the overarching matter of whether we can tune in to what I herein define as our *transmigration/elevation awareness*, to understand what this largely hidden and even denied <u>interdimensional out of body awareness and mobility instinct</u> actually is. This obvious and simple yet rather revolutionary tuning in involves our allowing ourselves to see/know that

Expansion, Elevation, Transmigration:
Survival Here And Beyond: Practices And Concepts

<u>transmigration/elevation is about the moving/migrating at will (of our awareness and thus of our non-physical selves) in and out of our physical bodies</u>. We can come to know whether and how we can, if needed, live/survive, for a time or for good, without our physical bodies and their biological brains (live as either a state of "mind" or in actuality as an awareness).

Note: We can think of our biological brain as a highly complex piece of equipment, a transmitter, designed to transmit our consciousness into the physical plane. The idea that our consciousness can exist out there without us, without our biological brain, is debated on an ongoing basis. Again, I note that whatever "side" of the debate we are on, there is another approach here, which is, as I indicate on these pages: We have the option to move beyond what we are now (or beyond what we believe ourselves to be now), <u>to develop</u> (or recognize): the capability of our consciousness <u>to assume further "say" in and control of its own evolution and capabilities</u>, including its non-physical survival.

Of course, among responses to this matter is the comment, "however, the consciousness requires the biological brain to collect and process its energy." Yet, the entire notion of the energy of a non-physical consciousness is open for debate as well, as: Consciousness itself, when/if existing non-physically, can appear as, or utilize, energy beyond means traditional science allows.

**It is time for us to
see BEYOND the definition of ourselves
as only biological life forms.
It is time to
SEE and REACH BEYOND.**

KEYS TO ACCESSING THE BEYOND

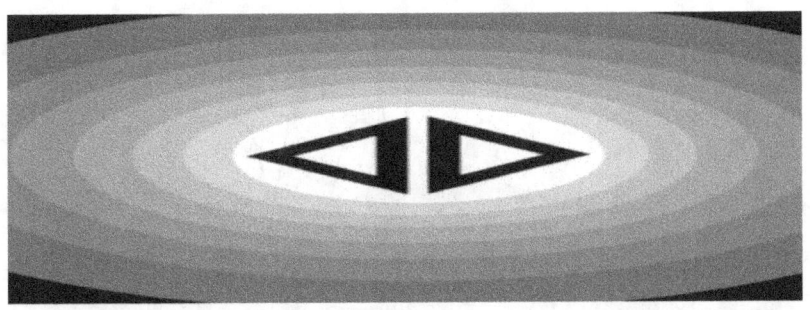

the truth about now

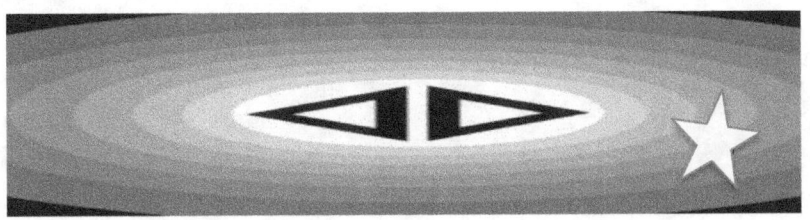

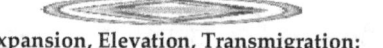
Expansion, Elevation, Transmigration:
Survival Here And Beyond: Practices And Concepts

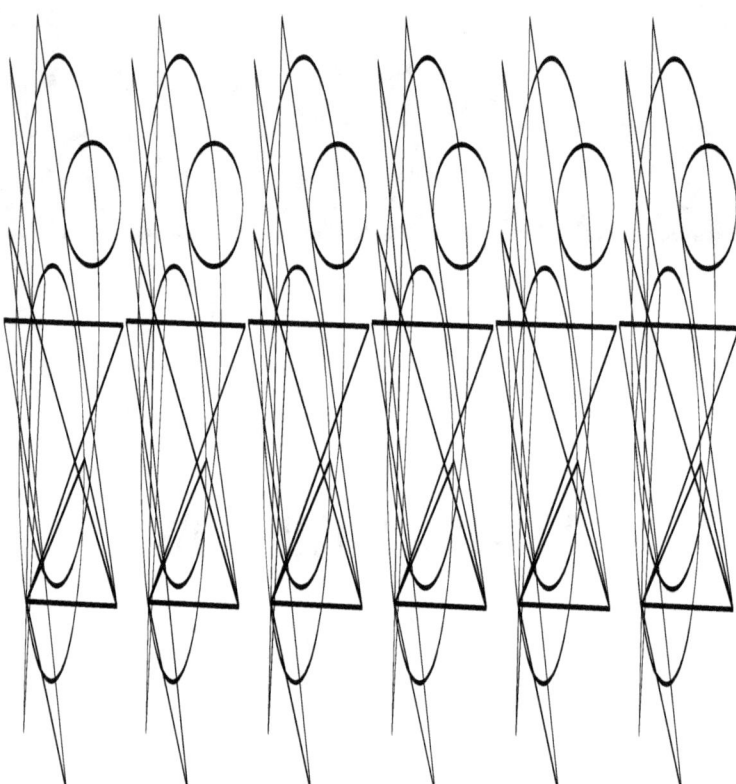

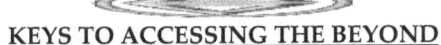

KEYS TO ACCESSING THE BEYOND

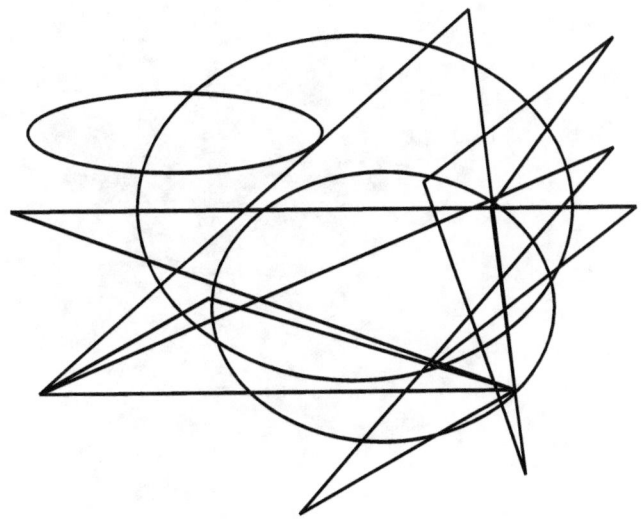

CHAPTER 2
Activate The Power Of Aware Knowing

KEY #2
BECOME AWARE OF AWARENESS ITSELF

αΩα

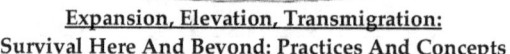
**Expansion, Elevation, Transmigration:
Survival Here And Beyond: Practices And Concepts**

Rising Sense Of Calm

When rising above (or beyond) the level of space, time, and reality we know, above or beyond physicality, above or beyond the level we see as where we live and as who we are...

There is a rising sense of calm, a general detachment, yet not a separation anxiety, nor a fear, not a sadness, rather simply an elevation out of the lower and more dense levels of emotions and ties to what we felt we were not only part of, but felt we were, felt our identities were.

And then, just when we are about to sense all is gone, that we are gone, **we find we still exist.** *Here is where the* **elevated identity** *can meet, can identify, can know, itself for who it truly is: ALIVE.*

Expansion, Elevation, Transmigration:
Survival Here And Beyond: Practices And Concepts

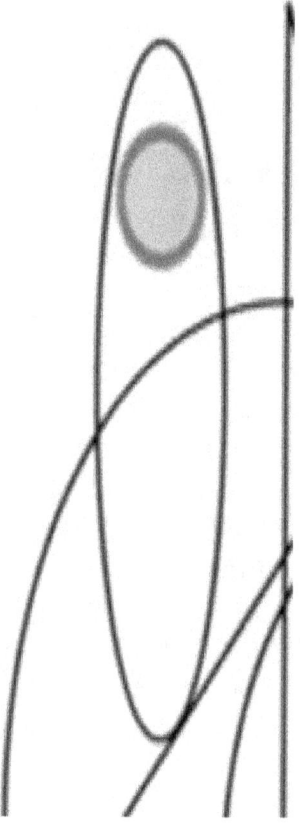

KEYS TO ACCESSING THE BEYOND

TRANSMIGRATION/ELEVATION INSTINCT: KEY #2

BECOME AWARE OF AWARENESS ITSELF

1) **Awareness,** while to some degree generally present in waking (and in other "lucid" and in other sleeping) life, is far more than what we tend to think of as awareness.
2) Awareness is a key element of consciousness. To become directly *aware of your consciousness*, begin with your awareness, grow ever more *aware of your awareness itself.*
3) Take a moment to focus on your awareness. This is not about focusing on what you are "aware *of,*" such as the person across the room, or the car racing down the street outside your window, or the cake baking in the oven. This is about being *aware of awareness itself.*
4) Sit with your awareness a while. No need to meditate or be hypnotized, or drug yourself. Simply say, "Hello awareness, I see you here, being aware of things taking place. Yet now I also see you here, *just being.*"
5) Feel yourself *aware of being aware* of non-physical and non-emotional essences. No need to define these, simply draw your awareness to what else there is to be aware of beyond the first sensations that race in (such as air temperature, hunger, physical desire, etc.).
6) This is a *self scan* for your levels of knowing and being beyond the explicit obvious emotional and physical realms. <u>Become increasingly aware of subtle presences and flows of non-physical seeming energies, whatever these seem to be to you.</u> Make notes on this. Do this scan once in a while, making notes on increasing awareness.

Expansion, Elevation, Transmigration:
Survival Here And Beyond: Practices And Concepts

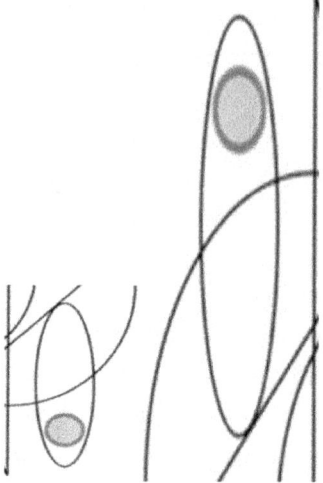

KEYS TO ACCESSING THE BEYOND

About This
TRANSMIGRATION / ELEVATION INSTINCT: KEY #2
BECOME AWARE OF AWARENESS ITSELF

Awareness is the "aware" and operant element of the consciousness. As simple as is the notion of awareness, this is a powerful resource we have yet to far more fully develop. Our heightened awareness itself will be key in our survival, will unveil, activate, and operate this essential transmigration /elevation instinct.

We are frequently calling upon ourselves to adjust, adapt, shift ourselves and our consciousness-es (via our awareness-es) from one perspective and dimension of ourselves to another. We may even at times sense that our psychological and even perhaps physical survival depends upon such a shift in our awareness. Of course, the challenge is to understand what this shift actually is, that this is not a physical relocation, rather a **shift in the acuity and focus of our awareness**.

Understanding what this shift is, that it is embedded in our own **transmigration instinct**, and how to facilitate this shift, can be key in our survival. We can open our minds, our consciousness-es, to their vast capacity to adjust, shift, move through and across dimensions of our lives, minds, realities. We can allow ourselves to think about the possibilities, about the concept of shifting in whatever form we choose.

This shifting is in essence what some will call a *"mental" exercise,* **what we best call a** *consciousness exercise,* **as the shift-elevate-expand (SEE) process I describe herein (in Key #5) takes place within and around,** *via,* **the awareness, even via the consciousness itself.**

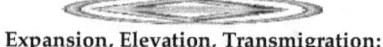

Expansion, Elevation, Transmigration:
Survival Here And Beyond: Practices And Concepts

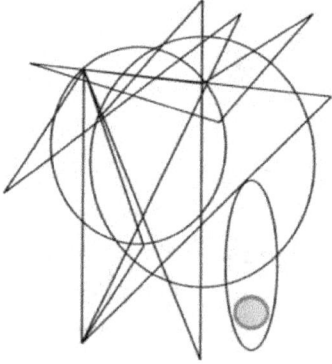

KEYS TO ACCESSING THE BEYOND

WE DO KNOW

We may at some point find a wide scale survival need to shift, to consciously engage in what I herein describe as the ***conscious transmigration/elevation*** of, ourselves across major views, beliefs, realities, dimensions, even perhaps, at least metaphorically, from physical to non-physical, or back and forth. It is therefore essential we have at least already explored, thought about, visualized, the metaphors, concepts, possibilities involved.

KEYS to minor and major *shift awareness-es* are shared in this book, made readily accessible for everyday coping as well as for potentially profound survival reasons. If we listen, we can hear ourselves and our species calling us. If we look closely, we can see ourselves reaching out to ourselves, telling us it is time to unveil, to know, what we carry deep within us:

the truth about ourselves:
the truth about now.

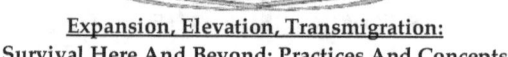

Expansion, Elevation, Transmigration:
Survival Here And Beyond: Practices And Concepts

This is about us.
Who we think we are.

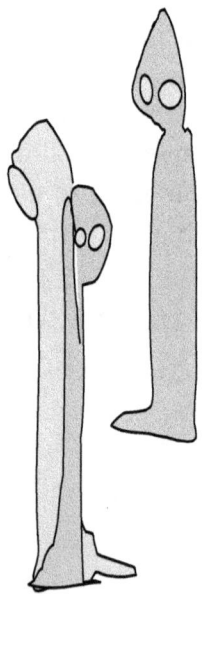

KEYS TO ACCESSING THE BEYOND

ABOUT ALL OF US

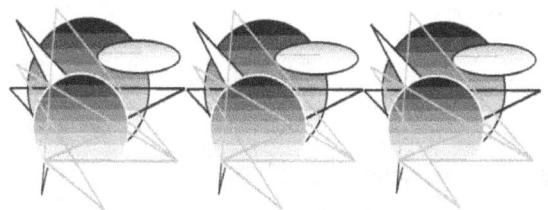

This is about all of us:

who we are as individuals,

who we are as a species,

who we are as a life form

inhabiting Earth's biosphere.

This is about what we know,
what we perceive,
what we are aware of....

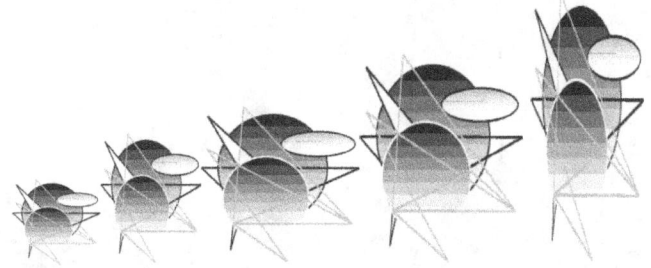

This involves our redefining ourselves, as what we have come to believe about who we are may have to amend itself. Our understanding of who we are and of what we are capable of has been formed, even dictated, by our biological brain's biological programming -- or by some other form affecting our knowing, suppressing the awareness functions of our consciousness.

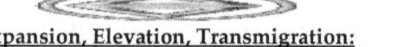

Expansion, Elevation, Transmigration:
Survival Here And Beyond: Practices And Concepts

WHO WE ARE CAN SURVIVE

YES.
This is about our consciousness,
**   our individual consciousness-es,**
**   and our collective consciousness.**

Who we are, rather than who we have been led to believe we are, is who can survive on in time....

KEYS TO ACCESSING THE BEYOND

These matters are quite profound…

The implications for us
as individuals, as a species, as an ecosystem, as a planet,
are quite profound,
and yet quite ordinary.

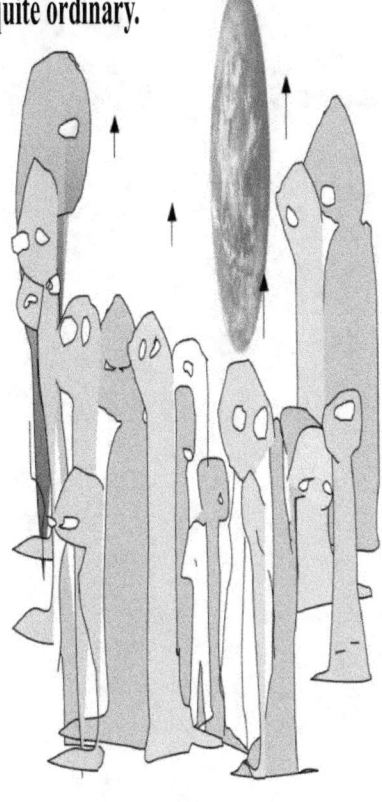

Expansion, Elevation, Transmigration:
Survival Here And Beyond: Practices And Concepts

KEYS TO ACCESSING THE BEYOND

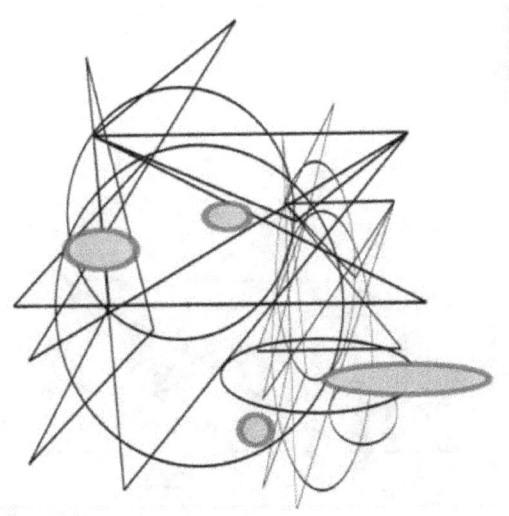

CHAPTER 3
Establish Your Focus: Identify Your SELF As Your Focal Point
(THIS WILL HELP SERVE AS A MARKER, A POINT OF IDENTITY IN NON-PHYSICAL SETTINGS)

KEY #3
SEE WHAT IS KEY IN TRANSMIGRATION
(FORM YOUR MARKER, YOUR POINT OF IDENTITY IN NON-PHYSICAL SETTINGS)

αΩα

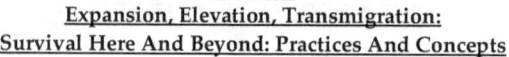
Expansion, Elevation, Transmigration:
Survival Here And Beyond: Practices And Concepts

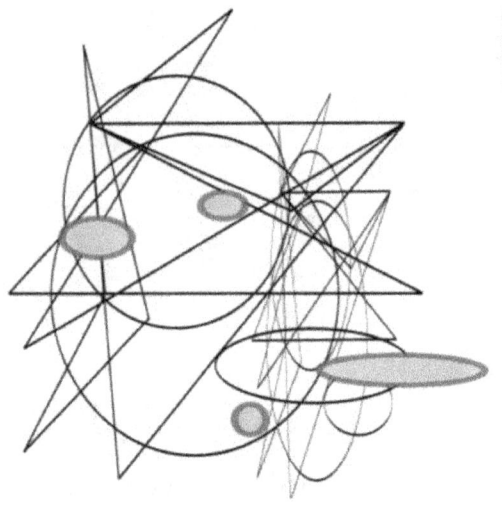

KEYS TO ACCESSING THE BEYOND

Once Simple Weightlessness

Hold on. Just be there, suspended. ...

What was a simple weightlessness now has its own gravity, a vague morph-less pulling so very inward, and yet out so very far, out beyond all the seeming edges: horizons fading, moving to and from themselves like waves. ... This emerging sense of gravity in this seeming weightlessness ebbs and flows, now glowing its own absorption, absorbing itself into the timelessness of the eternal now. Waiting, waiting, now you sense you see yourself in this space.

Then an always never ending-ness comes into its own space-less awareness. This newer ancient gravity beckons, calls the self, pulls to itself the self. Listen, as here you can hear yourself calling yourself to yourself. ... Here you are, still here. You can see this, even be this. You can stay you, re-coalescing to a self. Yes, you can stay you out here....

Expansion, Elevation, Transmigration:
Survival Here And Beyond: Practices And Concepts

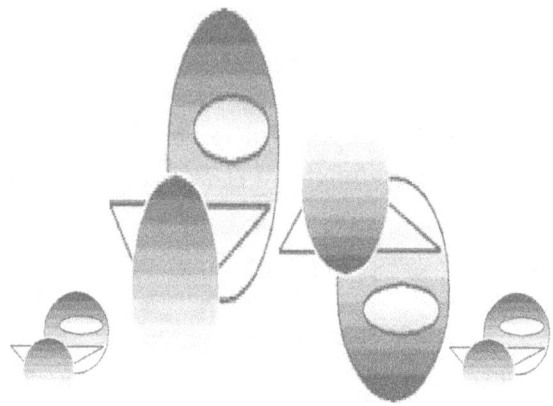

KEYS TO ACCESSING THE BEYOND

TRANSMIGRATION/ELEVATION INSTINCT: KEY #3

SEE WHAT IS KEY IN TRANSMIGRATION
(FORM YOUR MARKER,
YOUR POINT OF IDENTITY
IN NON-PHYSICAL SETTINGS)

1) Select a point within yourself. Give this a physical location to start with, perhaps your forehead. Begin to bring *your awareness* of yourself to this point.
2) Begin to identify your focus. Sense the presence of your focus within yourself. It may be distributed, perhaps scattered.
3) Sense *how aware you can be of your focus.* <u>See that your focus is your awareness consciously focusing itself.</u>
4) Feel you are aware of your focus. Now collect your focus to a central point, your FOCAL POINT (FP), within your consciousness.
5) Use your imagination to give your FOCAL POINT gravity, allowing this point to pull your focus to itself.
6) Sense your focus being more and more at this FOCAL POINT. Feel the sense of pull toward this point, a sort of gravitational pull by you toward you. Learn the feel of this FOCAL POINT, the sensations it offers you, identifies itself as being.
7) Know your FOCAL POINT more and more. Become ever more familiar with, AWARE OF, this FOCAL POINT, as this is YOU. Your focal point is your awareness. You are this awareness. Make notes on the evolution of your awareness, and on how you can more and more draw your awareness to your focal point.

Expansion, Elevation, Transmigration:
Survival Here And Beyond: Practices And Concepts

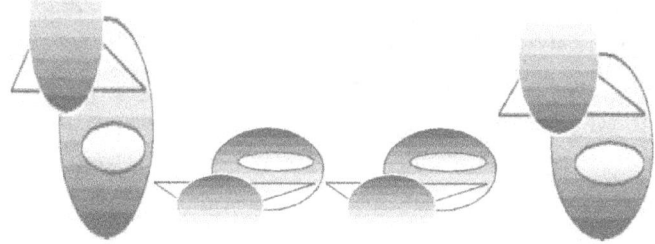

KEYS TO ACCESSING THE BEYOND

About This
TRANSMIGRATION / ELEVATION INSTINCT: KEY #3
SEE WHAT IS KEY IN TRANSMIGRATION:
  ESTABLISH YOUR FOCUS,
  IDENTIFY YOURSELF AS YOUR FOCAL POINT.
  THIS WILL HELP SERVE AS
  YOUR MARKER, YOUR POINT OF IDENTITY
  IN NON-PHYSICAL SETTINGS

This book, KEYS TO ACCESSING THE BEYOND, offers KEYS (steps, processes, awareness-es) to accessing what is there for us – and or for <u>developing what can be there for us</u> once we know this can be there:

THE BEYOND.

PREPARE YOUR WAY

This BEYOND is a state of mind and is a territory. This BEYOND is a place we already do exist in, and can live within. This BEYOND is right here right now, in what for many are the unseen or even unrecognized areas of the mind, heart, and soul.

Many will think of this BEYOND as the place of the after-life. Some will even call this BEYOND heaven. And certainly, understanding and even learning about ACCESSING THE BEYOND now, while still in a physical biological body, is valuable and can provide useful awareness and experience for a later time when you may not be in a physical body, and still want to survive "out there."

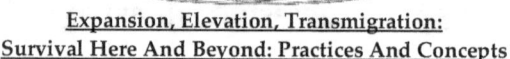

<u>Expansion, Elevation, Transmigration:
Survival Here And Beyond: Practices And Concepts</u>

By "out there" I am referring to what is or may be BEYOND physicality, BEYOND the material plane – outside this three-D (3-D) dimension. I am also referring to what can be there for us once we leave our biological bodies with their biological brains: THE BEYOND. I say *can be there for us*, as we can develop this place, this domain, this territory, once we understand that KEY TO ACCESSING THIS TERRITORY is knowing it can exist – that we can actually develop this for ourselves.

THINK OF HOW MANY TIMES
YOU WERE LOOKING FOR SOMETHING
AND DID NOT SEE IT RIGHT THERE IN FRONT OF YOU,
AS YOU DID NOT KNOW TO LOOK FOR IT
OR HOW TO ACCESS IT.

THE KEY TO (THE TECHNOLOGY OF) THIS ACCESS

We can think of the KEYS TO ACCESSING THE BEYOND as a technology, a technology of the mind, yes, more so a technology of the awareness, still more so a technology of the consciousness. We can develop for ourselves the *tools of this access* that can work for us. Each of us will adapt the KEYS TO ACCESSING THE BEYOND to ourselves, to our belief systems, to our mental and even emotional and even spiritual views.

Central in developing KEYS TO ACCESSING THE BEYOND is developing the awareness, <u>the conscious awareness</u>, of these KEYS and of their steps and processes, even of their sensations (which for some will be parallel to lucid dream, out of body, and near death type experiences and their sensations).

KEYS TO ACCESSING THE BEYOND

Most central in all this is the sense of the SELF as a SELF that exists, <u>or can learn to exist,</u> both in physicality and BEYOND physicality.

**Here is where there can be
an ever deepening sense of
the expanded SELF,
the interdimensional SELF who is the actual SELF.**

**To address this actual SELF, <u>the SELF who can survive,</u>
this KEYS TO ACCESSING THE BEYOND book
develops a**
<u>technology of the SELF.</u>

**This SELF is not the ego-defined SELF,
not the product of the surface or even what some call
the deep psychology.
This SELF is located far more deeply into the being,
deeply seated and seeded in the
core of
the conscious awareness.**

Note, as per the TECHNOLOGY OF SELF detailed (for example) in the **TRANSMIGRATION / ELEVATION INSTINCT: KEY #3** at the opening of this chapter:

The *identity of*, even the *sense of*, <u>SELF,</u> can begin to (re)perceive itself as the <u>*awareness pulls to its focal point*</u>, FP -- rather than simply continuing to see itself as, or confuse its identity with, the physical vehicle/body it has been wearing or traveling in.

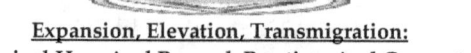

<u>Expansion, Elevation, Transmigration:</u>
<u>Survival Here And Beyond: Practices And Concepts</u>

***

The more we recognize ourselves as who we truly are, the more we know that **who we are can learn to survive**. It may be rather unusual to say it this way, yet in this book we can become more clear about this:

As we more and more know ourselves, we more and more know who it is that may be surviving when we survive.

ALSO AMONG THESE KEYS,
THESE SURVIVAL TOOLS,
ARE
THE COMPASSION EFFECTS

Note: We can begin to sense ourselves, even to better be in touch with our own identity, as we experience an acknowledgment of ourselves from ourselves. This acknowledgement includes the experience of compassion for ourselves, something many find far easier to give others than to give themselves.

KEYS TO ACCESSING THE BEYOND

THE CHOICE

We of the Human Species have a choice: THE choice to **dramatically SHIFT our evolutionary journey**.

This shift in our evolutionary path and speed can be conducted, fueled, by our own Human Consciousness. Indeed, it is our assuming conscious control of our own evolution that can make the difference in…
> **our suvival here on Earth
> and in this cosmos.**

Key to our mental, even physical, survival may indeed be the capabilities of our consciousness to **shift our…**
- **awareness and its:**
- **focus**
- **presence**
- **locus.**

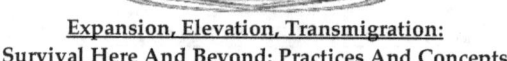

<u>Expansion, Elevation, Transmigration:
Survival Here And Beyond: Practices And Concepts</u>

UNDERSTAND THE UNTAPPED

Understanding the as yet untapped in full ... capabilities and capacities of our consciousness ... is essential now.

**We carry within us
keys to unlock doors,
gateways,
passages to domains,
niches,
we have a right to know,
<u>and a right to access.</u>**

**Knowing more and more
of our own consciousness
is itself a big step
in accessing
what lies
BEYOND.**

KEYS TO ACCESSING THE BEYOND

Knowing who and what we actually are may be key to our long term survival. Has this truth been suppressed or coded out of our awareness?

> **Would we know?**
> **Would our brains**
> **allow us to know?**
>
> **Or do our brains naturally**
> **wall out this knowing?**

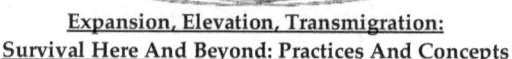

Expansion, Elevation, Transmigration:
Survival Here And Beyond: Practices And Concepts

FOR OUR CONSCIOUSNESS TO BE FREE STANDING, INDEPENDENT OF OUR BIOLOGY, INDEPENDENT OF OUR BIOLOGICAL BRAIN,

we must understand what this means.

For us to be able to SHIFT ourselves,
our consciousness-es,
from being bound to our biology to
being independent of our biology,
we must realize what it means to be
<u>free standing</u> ...

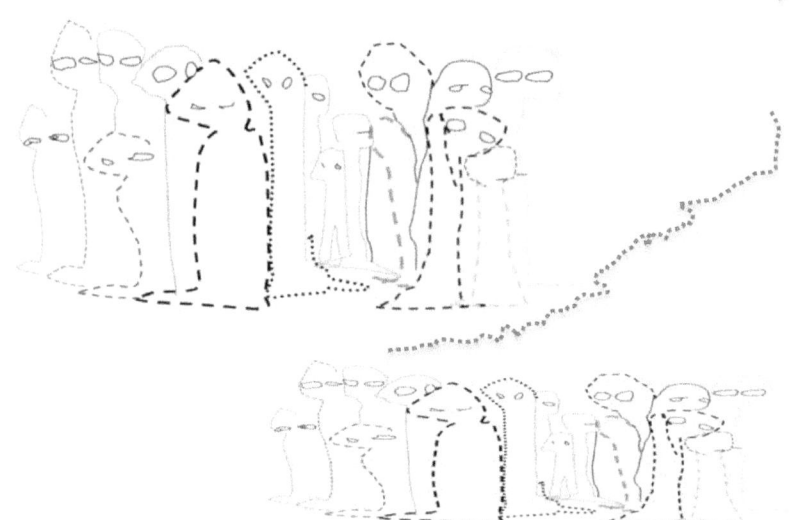

... rather than
tied to biology
to exist, to live, to survive.

KEYS TO ACCESSING THE BEYOND

WE HUMANS CAN NOW CONSCIOUSLY...

assume our rightful place in our own evolution.

This involves our bringing forth the magnificent and vast capacities of the CONSCIOUSNESS OF OUR HUMAN SPECIES.

We can assume a conscious role in our species' evolution process, even in the evolution of our Human brain.

This stepping forward to assume our rightful role in our own evolution, in the evolution of the capacities and reaches of our own Human Consciousness, may be at some point essential to our individual as well as species survival.

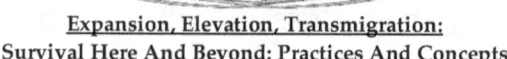

Expansion, Elevation, Transmigration:
Survival Here And Beyond: Practices And Concepts

ACCESSING OURSELVES

<u>Accessing</u> the full range of ourselves, of our consciousness, to survive, may have been limited via accidental event, or by our biological evolution, or perhaps even via purposeful intervention.

However these possible limits were formed, placed, inserted, implanted into our evolution, we can break free of these limits now.

<u>We can and perhaps must break free
to have a real say in the
survival of our selves and of our species.</u>

These limits may not even be actual,
yet may be *perceived limits*,
with these coded-in perceptions
somehow set, implanted,
within us, within our species
to control us,
to hold us back from ...

**our interdimensional potential
and our interdimensional survival options.**

KEYS TO ACCESSING THE BEYOND

CONSIDER FOR A MOMENT

Consider for a moment
just the possibility that
an intelligent designer of some form
actually has designed us, our species,
our biological brains and bodies,
to be genetically coded
not to know …

what
our true capabilities are…
what our magnificent consciousness-es are actually capable of…

not to know who we Humans actually are ---
not to know we can actually ACCESS THE BEYOND ---
and or generate a BEYOND for ourselves.

WE ARE NOT ONLY BIOLOGICAL

What if we Humans
are more than
we have been able to,
or allowed to,
or allowed ourselves to,
see that we are:

<u>**a species of consciousness
rather than only a mere biological life form.**</u>

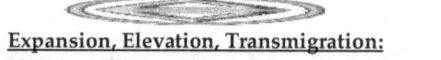

Expansion, Elevation, Transmigration:
Survival Here And Beyond: Practices And Concepts

This may at first be bewildering because we have been led to believe* in limitations which are not actual...

*may have even been brainwashed into believing....

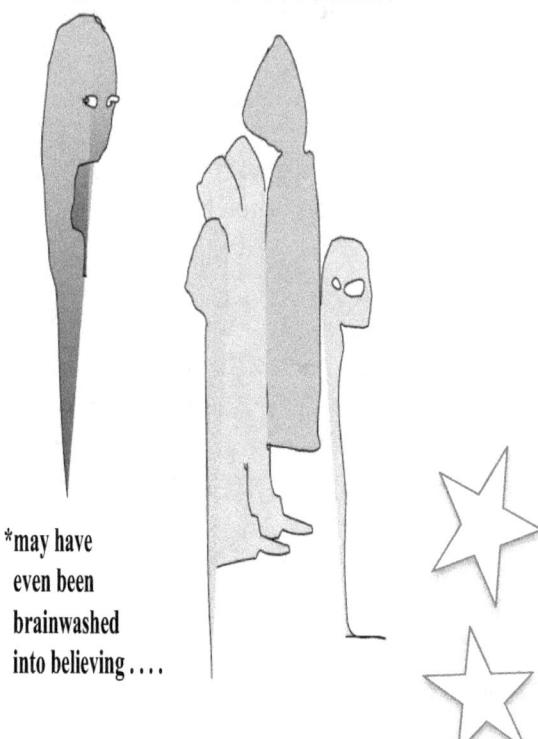

KEYS TO ACCESSING THE BEYOND

The whole picture is actually quite obvious, actually a reality whose time has come:

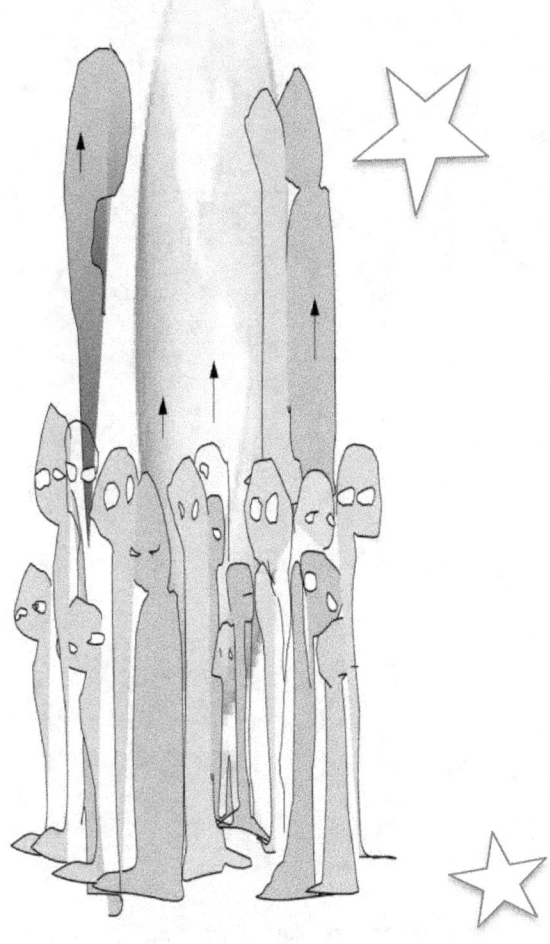

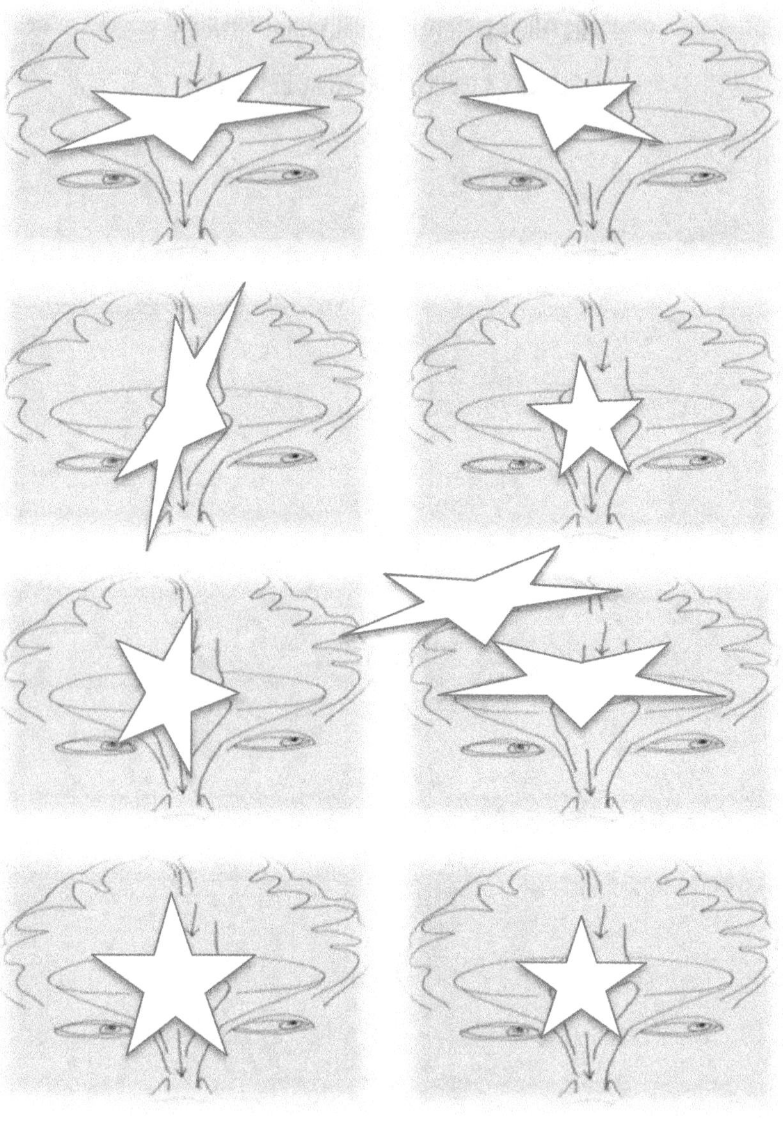

Expansion, Elevation, Transmigration:
Survival Here And Beyond: Practices And Concepts

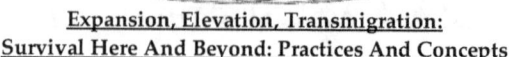

THE MULTI-MIND SEES MORE THAN WE KNOW

KEYS TO ACCESSING THE BEYOND

CHAPTER 4
We Must Be Able To Expand To New Places

KEY #4
DEVELOP / ENHANCE AFPL = AWARENESS-FOCUS-PRESENCE-LOCUS

$\alpha\Omega\alpha$

Expansion, Elevation, Transmigration:
Survival Here And Beyond: Practices And Concepts

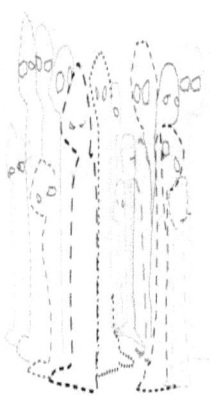

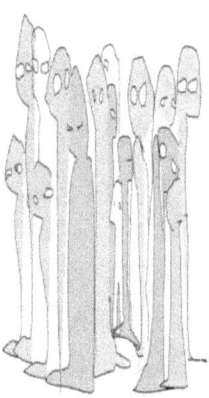

KEYS TO ACCESSING THE BEYOND

Face To Face

Face to face with the sense that our species' survival here on this Earth may at some point be at risk, we come to know there are real limits to what our physicality can do for us.

We can come to see that our survival may depend upon our redefining what and who we are –

and what it is that can truly survive profoundly changing physical environments and conditions.

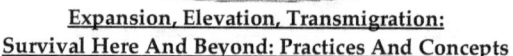

Expansion, Elevation, Transmigration:
Survival Here And Beyond: Practices And Concepts

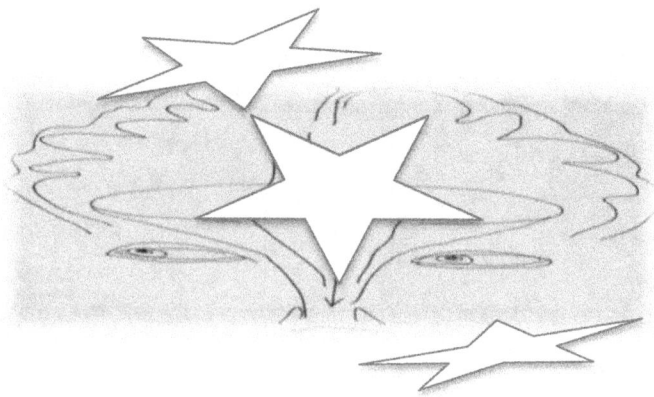

KEYS TO ACCESSING THE BEYOND

TRANSMIGRATION ELEVATION INSTINCT: KEY #4

DEVELOP / ENHANCE AFPL = AWARENESS-FOCUS-PRESENCE-LOCUS

1) AWARENESS
Become aware of the sense of knowing, of being, that you are experiencing. Find sensations you associate with this <u>awareness</u>, read these throughout your body, then throughout your BBS self, your beyond (physical) body sensation SELF. As you do, begin to sense, be ever more aware of, both your IN body and your OUT of body awareness and its focus, presence, locus....

2) FOCUS
Select a point in your body or yourself you can choose to focus on. Begin to pull the sensations of your awareness toward this point, your <u>FOCAL POINT</u>.

3) PRESENCE
As your awareness pulls into this one point, this point of focus, begin to feel the strength, <u>THE PRESENCE</u>, of this focus at this one point.

4) LOCUS
For now, identify your SELF with THE IDEA OF this one point, this point of FOCUS, this FOCAL POINT (FP). Begin to sense this is your current <u>LOCUS</u>, the place and space where you, where who you are, your awareness, can be at will, whether or not you are actually in your physical biological body.

■■

Note: Practicing this AFPL Exercise while you live in a physical biological body will allow you to become familiar with this identification and location of your awareness and thus consciousness, of who you are -- even when you have left your physical body. This will allow you to know yourself more and more in non-physical realms as well as on the physical plane, and to recognize that you have focus, presence, and location options both here and BEYOND.

Expansion, Elevation, Transmigration:
Survival Here And Beyond: Practices And Concepts

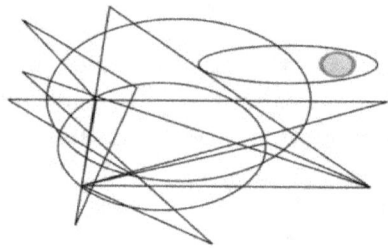

KEYS TO ACCESSING THE BEYOND

<u>About</u>
TRANSMIGRATION ELEVATION INSTINCT: KEY #4
DEVELOP / ENHANCE AFPL =
AWARENESS-FOCUS-PRESENCE-LOCUS

We can become more and more aware of, sensitized to, our location in time and space. We can be constantly – even if simply in the back our our mind -- generating a sense of ourselves as non-physical beings moving through non-physical realities, without physical bodies.

This is ever more consciously being aware of our own state of mind -- or better stated, state of awareness level. Fine tuning our awareness allows us to consciously sense how aware we are at any given moment, how consciously aware we are – aware that we are aware.

**As we ever more consciously fine tune our awareness,
we can then consciously fine tune our focus.**

**As we ever more consciously fine tune our focus,
we can then consciously fine tune our presence.**

**As we ever more consciously fine tune our presence,
we can then consciously fine tune our locus –
our location itself – both here and BEYOND.**

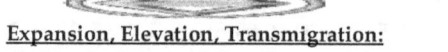

Expansion, Elevation, Transmigration:
Survival Here And Beyond: Practices And Concepts

Become aware of the <u>sense of knowing you exist</u> -- the <u>sense of being</u> that you are experiencing. Find sensations you associate with this <u>awareness</u>, read these throughout your body, then throughout your BBS self, your beyond (physical) body sensation SELF. As you do, begin to sense, be ever more aware of, both your IN body and your OUT of body awareness and its focus, presence, locus....

Choose a point on your body. For now, identify your SELF with this one point, this point of FOCUS, this FOCAL POINT (FP). Begin to sense this is your LOCUS, the place and space where you, who you are, your awareness, can be at will, whether or not you are in your physical body.

YOU CAN LEARN TO DO THIS BY PRACTICING THIS AT DIFFERENT FOCAL POINTS YOU SELECT BOTH IN AND OUTSIDE YOUR PHYSICAL BIOLOGICAL BODY.

■ ■

Note: Practicing this while you live in a physical (biological) body is an excellent learning opportunity. This will allow you to become ever more familiar with this identification and location of your awareness and of your consciousness, of your SELF -- <u>of who you are when you have left your physical body</u> – and of that you are, that you exist, when you have <u>left your physical body.</u> **This will allow you to know yourself when you meet your SELF in non-physical realms -- to recognize that you have location options, and to see that you survived, you have ACCESSED THE BEYOND.**

> ***
>
> Note: This is how we can learn to move ourselves through spaces we cannot and do not define from a physical, material, plane standpoint. This is how we learn to expand, to transmigrate, to be moving to and from, back and forth between, the material plane and the BEYOND of non-physicality.

KEYS TO ACCESSING THE BEYOND

**We have the right to, and
we must
evolve, expand, reach into
A NEW NICHE**

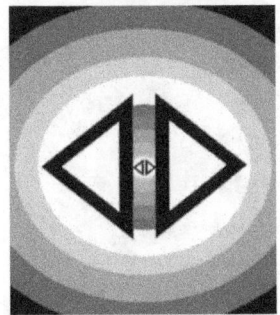

**live in but also beyond,
(be able to travel to and from)...**

**...to and from
our present niche to a new niche.**

We can now understand, be conscious of, the option our consciousness-es themselves can offer us, which is to be able to shift, to "elevate," from mental state to mental state, from psychological place to psychological place, from physical niche to physical niche or non-physical niche, from one dimension of our reality to another dimension of our reality, to transmigrate.

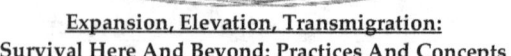

Expansion, Elevation, Transmigration:
Survival Here And Beyond: Practices And Concepts

IT IS TIME

Indeed, the time has come,
the time must be here now
for the sake of our survival,

for us to consciously (re)activate
our conscious ability to elevate:
to shift our awareness-es,
to shift our perceptions,
to shift ourselves,
in order to travel in and out of,
<u>even prepare to inhabit</u>,

new niches of
our minds and our realities,
new niches in
our physical plane,
maybe even new niches
outside this biosphere on Earth…
perhaps even
beyond this physical dimension.

KEYS TO ACCESSING THE BEYOND

POSSIBILITIES ARE HERE FOR US TO SEE.

Our own consciousness carries these possibilities....

We must . . .

INHABIT MORE THAN JUST

this thing we think is our reality:

this thing, the physical plane.

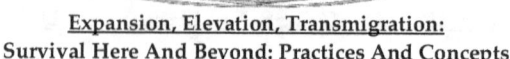

Expansion, Elevation, Transmigration:
Survival Here And Beyond: Practices And Concepts

PREPARE TO INHABIT

We must be prepared to inhabit, at least in concept, for now as metaphor, perhaps at some point in actuality, more than this physical "plane" Earth niche.

>We must be able to do so,
>in case at some time we need to do so.

>We must understand the
>capacity of our consciousness to shift,
>to move along the interdimensional META-AXIS,
>TO FOCUS OURSELVES
>TO SEE THE LEAP
>WE CAN MAKE,
>to *adapt* by making
>dimensionally mobile
>our awareness,
>our energy,
>our selves,
>our species.

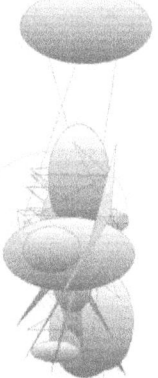

This is a simple understanding, as we know this: deep within ourselves we know who we are, we know the power of our consciousness.

KEYS TO ACCESSING THE BEYOND

As a species aware of risks to its well-being in this Earth's biosphere, we can do everything possible to save this, our Earthly habitat...and to save ourselves as well, whether this be here in this Earth habitat, or elsewhere, even BEYOND.

Expansion, Elevation, Transmigration:
Survival Here And Beyond: Practices And Concepts

KEYS TO ACCESSING THE BEYOND

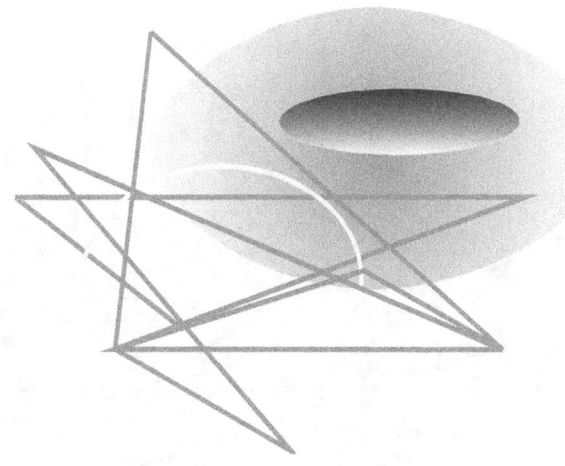

CHAPTER 5
We Can Be Truly Mobile To Truly Survive

KEY #5
NOW SEE THE SEE =
THE SHIFT ELEVATE EXPAND
TRANSFORMATION

αΩα

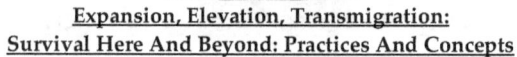
Expansion, Elevation, Transmigration:
Survival Here And Beyond: Practices And Concepts

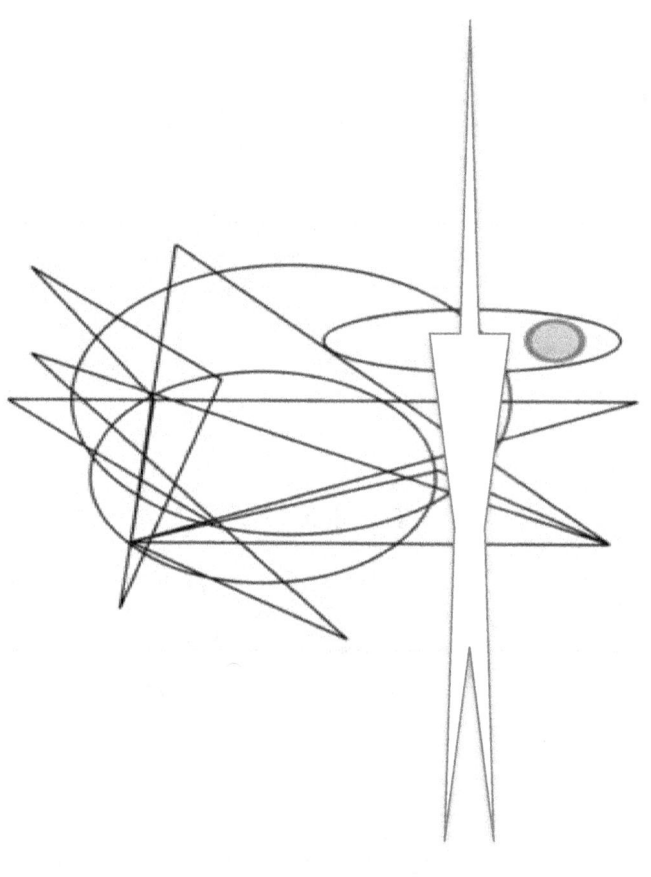

KEYS TO ACCESSING THE BEYOND

Capability We Do Have

A growing expansion of being,
an un-grounding,
a lightening of presence, an ability to …
move, change, re-form, reconstitute…
all this is the elevating,
the shifting sense, the shifting instinct and capability
we can come to know we carry within ourselves.

The shift is a capability we do have.
On a deep level, we know what shifting is.
We understand this
use of metaphor, of imagination,
this form of <u>conceptual transit</u>,
of transformative process and action.

Shifting is already underway.
Becoming conscious of
this shifting can allow us to captain
our processes, journeys,
evolutions,
as these are ours –
once we assume our actual
identity as
the consciousness we are.

Expansion, Elevation, Transmigration:
Survival Here And Beyond: Practices And Concepts

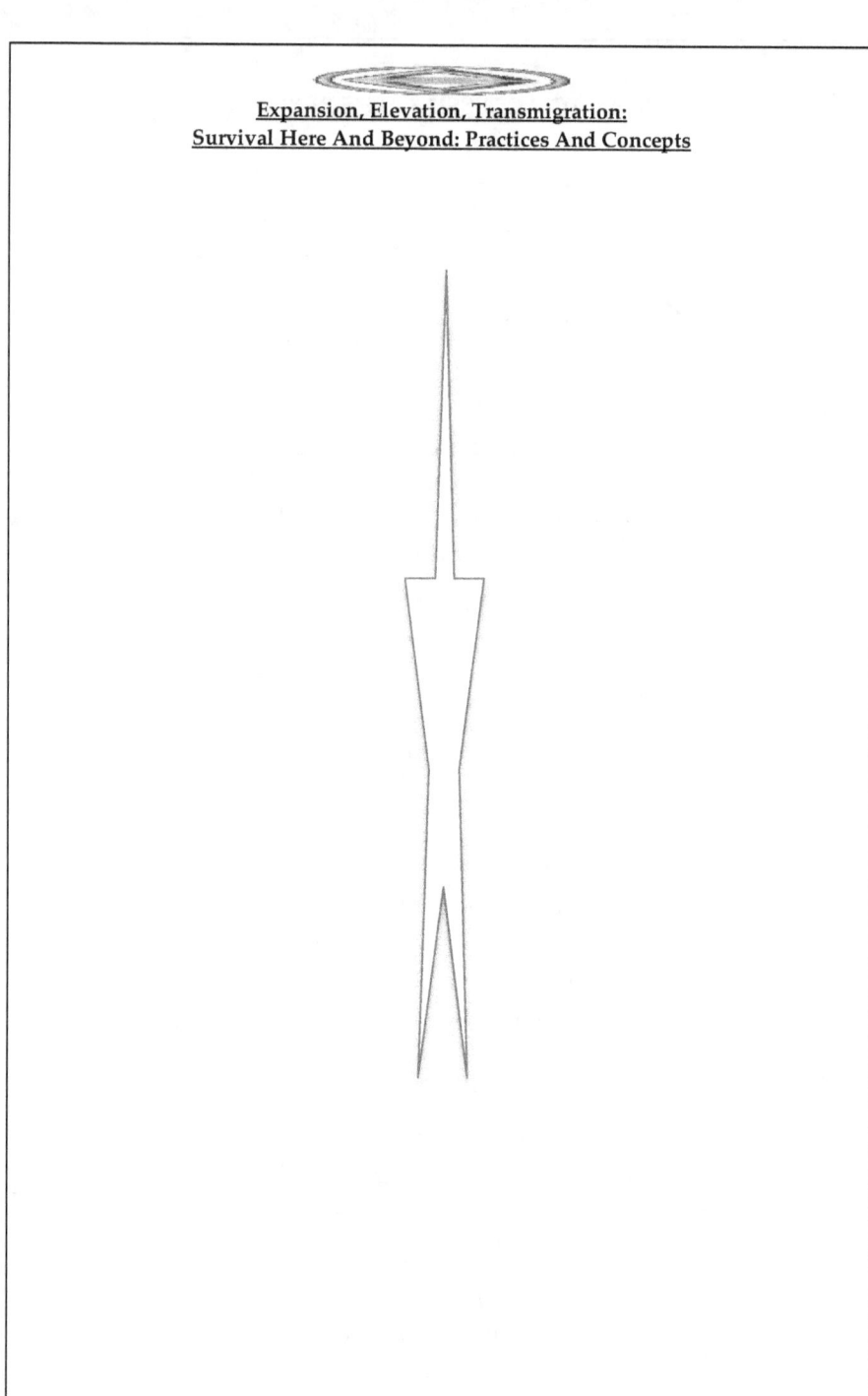

KEYS TO ACCESSING THE BEYOND

TRANSMIGRATION/ELEVATION INSTINCT: KEY #5

NOW SEE THE SEE =
THE SHIFT ELEVATE EXPAND TRANSFORMATION

1) You may at some time have said something like, "I can just *see* myself in that hat, or that shirt, or that car, or that job, or that place."
2) Take a moment to see yourself now, see yourself somewhere else, such as across town, or in a jet on a trip. Become aware of what this seeing yourself somewhere feels like.
3) Notice that your imagination is seeing yourself somewhere else, is *imagining, visualizing/imaging*--you are in another environment or location.
4) Practice imagining that you are somewhere else. Begin by choosing places you feel you know. Notice what is going on in your awareness as you do this. No need to define this process in specific words, simply sense the experience you are having, be *aware of your awareness* of this.
5) Once you feel familiar with the inner process of seeing yourself somewhere, begin to imagine seeing yourself in less familiar environments, places and spaces where you perhaps float or fly or feel beyond the physical plane, whatever this may feel like for you.
6) As you do this, imagine yourself moving away from Earth's gravity, shifting into another environment, and into another form of yourself that can be in that environment. Give yourself a direction such as "upward," and "elevate" yourself in that direction. As you do, begin to fill the space you are in, expand into this space.
7) Be here for a while. No need to define this or force this, just notice this, become familiar with this experience. Make notes on this later.

Expansion, Elevation, Transmigration:
Survival Here And Beyond: Practices And Concepts

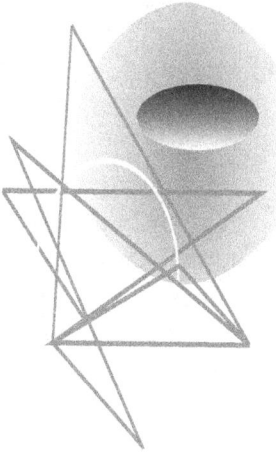

KEYS TO ACCESSING THE BEYOND

**About this
TRANSMIGRATION / ELEVATION INSTINCT: KEY #5**
*NOW SEE THE <u>SEE</u> =
THE SHIFT ELEVATE EXPAND TRANSFORMATION*

Being able to consciously move through situations involves being as conscious of what is going on as we can be. Of course, this may be easier said than done. After all, how can we see **all** or **even most of** what is affecting us? Being increasingly conscious of what we do not fully see may involve:

> **making room in our mind and brain
> for the IDEA that there are
> spaces, realms, territories of our mind,
> of our SELF,
> where we can work with
> what may seem
> invisible or difficult to see,
> such as subtle
> developments, events, trends, and patterns.**

Finding our way through minor and major changes and transitions involves our being able to <u>see</u> what may be affecting, or slowing, or even distorting, our process, perhaps tying us to patterns that must shift or change or end.

Moving through complex situations and patterns involves being able to <u>see</u> these situations and patterns as energetic networks, webs of cordings and attachments. We can continue <u>to fine tune our awareness to allow us to see, to sense, to hear, to know,</u> more about what is going on within and around us. We can sensitize ourselves to know more about what energy networks we are enmeshed in.

Expansion, Elevation, Transmigration:
Survival Here And Beyond: Practices And Concepts

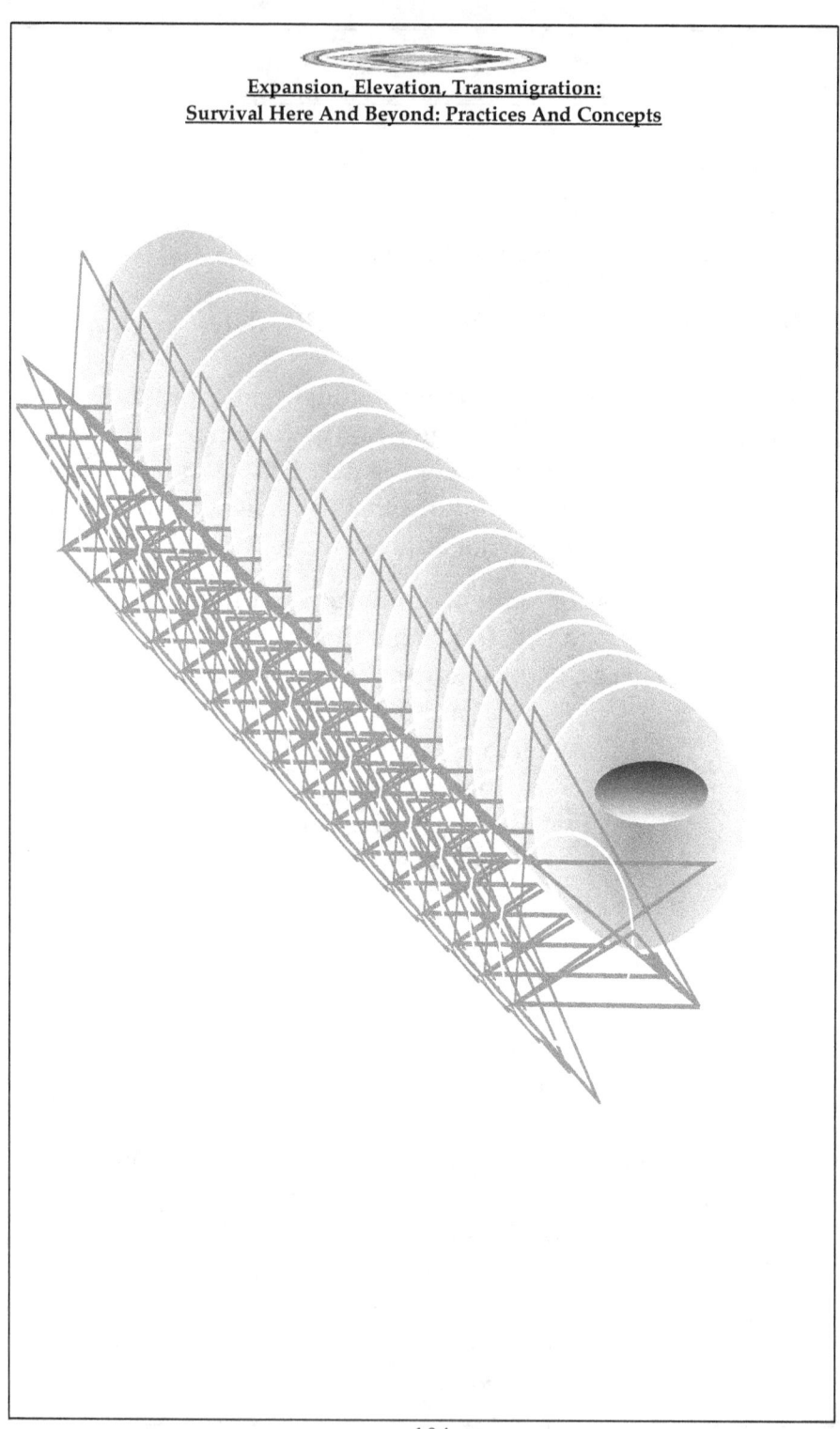

KEYS TO ACCESSING THE BEYOND

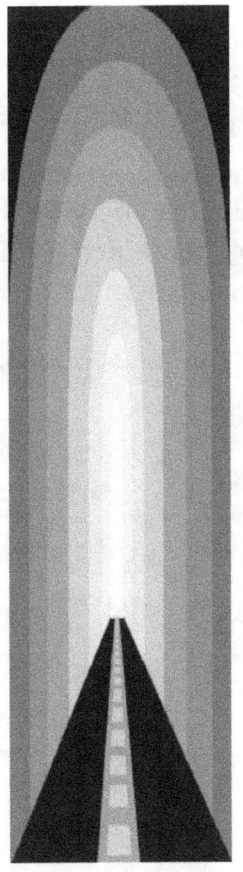

This is about seeing
ourselves as

INTERDIMENSIONALLY

MOBILE

and understanding that this
inter dimensional mobility
is quite natural
and
is our birthright.

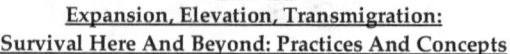

Expansion, Elevation, Transmigration:
Survival Here And Beyond: Practices And Concepts

WE CAN BEGIN BY REALIZING

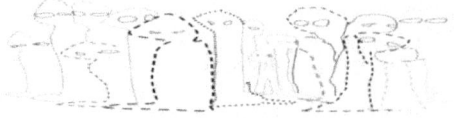

We can begin by realizing the vast interdimensional awareness and capability of ourselves as individuals, and as a species, and as a <u>species consciousness</u>, which is who we are: a species of consciousness.

Our accessing this vast awareness and capability involves our realizing we are indeed ...

members of

<u>a species of consciousness
rather than simply a
biological life form.</u>

OUR SPECIES ALREADY LIVES
BOTH HERE AND BEYOND.

WE CAN CONSCIOUSLY SHIFT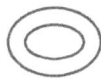

This book, KEYS TO ACCESSING THE BEYOND, says that survival BEYOND biological existence can be developed, evolved, learned, practiced. This is about the opportunity we have to be here in the material plane as a biological life form, and to also be reaching BEYOND where we may at some time be without our biological body.

So this is about what I suggest is our natural mobility, our natural ability to reach BEYOND, even while still living in a biological body, as well as after this biological life.

The natural conscious interdimensional mobility I am suggesting here is the capability of our awareness to move itself, to shift, from one habitat to another, from one state of awareness to another, from one dimension to another, for example, from physical to non-physical, and back and forth from these states of being and awareness.

Once we understand that all shifts of focus and perceived locus (location, place) are in essence the product of our consciousness, then we can consciously shift to survive.

THIS IS THE WAY WE CAN SEE OURSELVES ALREADY IN THE PROCESS OF TRANSFORMATION.

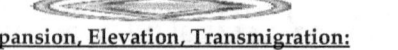

**Expansion, Elevation, Transmigration:
Survival Here And Beyond: Practices And Concepts**

I am suggesting that this further developed inter-dimensional consciousness thinking and mobility is the next step in our INDIVIDUAL AND SPECIES SURVIVAL BOTH HERE AND BEYOND.

This step, this conscious shift in our thinking and awareness, in our consciousness itself, is both a small step and a big step, and is also step of a most

revolutionary nature.

KEYS TO ACCESSING THE BEYOND

OPTIONS OF PROFOUND PROPORTIONS

We will come to understand we have
<u>survival options of profound proportions.</u>

These are options
we have not yet entirely
foreseen
or perhaps have been
prevented from foreseeing...
have been prevented by
particular evolutionary events and or errors, or by forces intervening in our evolution, perhaps via some form of implant externally directing our evolution,
or by other intelligent design.

Nevertheless, we can break through whatever may have been impeding our knowing, to find the true nature and capacity of our species, of our expansive individual and species consciousness ... and

>to unveil this instinct we carry,
>>this instinct to access our rightful
>>>- interdimensional survival awareness
>>- **TO ACCESS THE BEYOND --**
>>>>**OUR BEYOND.**

Expansion, Elevation, Transmigration:
Survival Here And Beyond: Practices And Concepts

We can SEE and make profound LEAPs in awareness, and corresponding still more profound ...
interdimensional LEAPs.

Readers, I have defined the LEAP I speak of here as the
light-energy-action-process.
I define the SEE as the
shift-elevate-expand
(expansion transformation).

This is the core of the herein defined
TRANSMIGRATION-ELEVATION
TECHNOLOGY,
the recipe for METAXIS or the
META-AXIS, the interdimensional shift
of our awareness and its focal point.
I explain the
METAXIS as
TRANSMIGRATIONAL ELEVATION,
and a series of
TRANSMIGRATIONS (ELEVATION SHIFTS),
as being
TRANSMIGRATIONAL METAXES.

Note: What is shifting here is the consciousness and its awareness, with this shifting taking place via focus of the awareness and energy of the consciousness. The ease of this transmigration is facilitated by the non-physical essence or "lightness of being" that is itself transmigration/elevation.

KEYS TO ACCESSING THE BEYOND

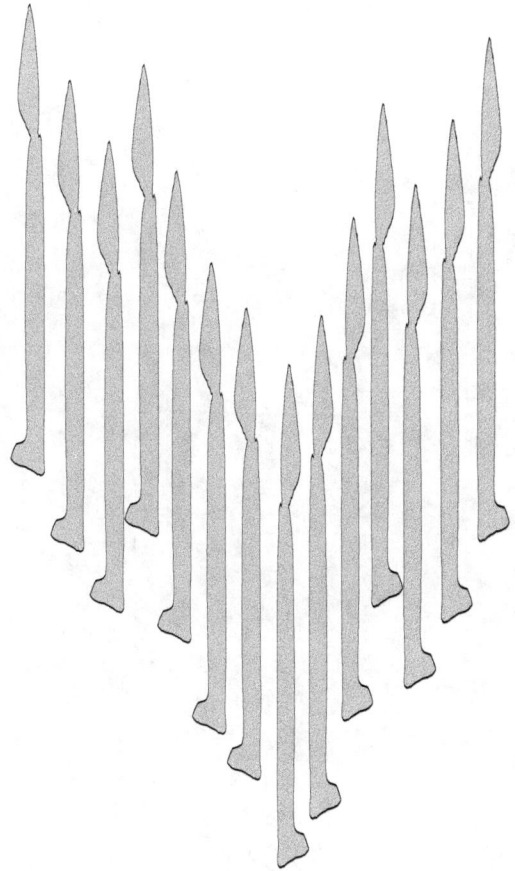

DIMENSIONAL EXPANSION FOR SURVIVAL

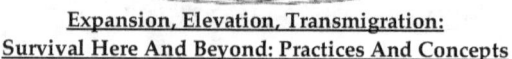
Expansion, Elevation, Transmigration:
Survival Here And Beyond: Practices And Concepts

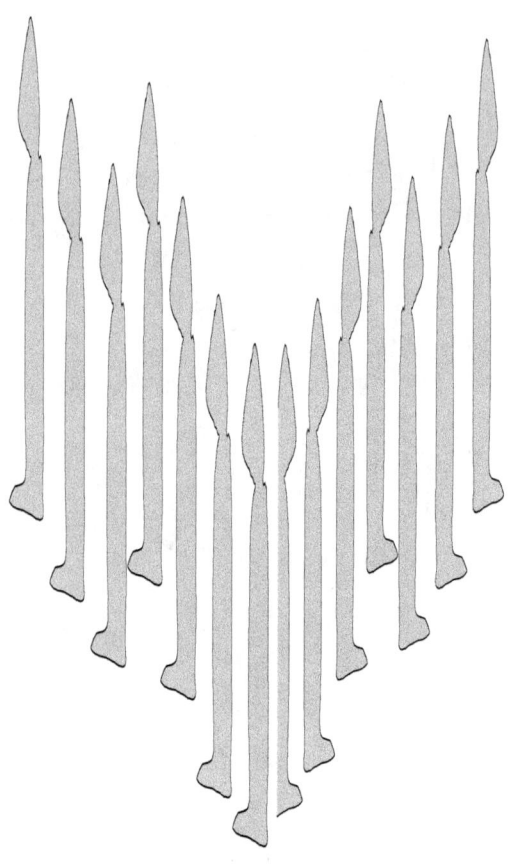

KEYS TO ACCESSING THE BEYOND

CHAPTER 6
We Are Already Equipped To Expand, Elevate, Transmigrate

KEY #6
KNOW THE LEAP =
THE LIGHT ENERGY ACTION PROCESS

αΩα

Expansion, Elevation, Transmigration:
Survival Here And Beyond: Practices And Concepts

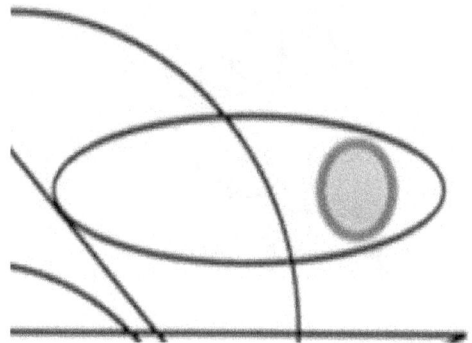

KEYS TO ACCESSING THE BEYOND

Sensing We Are Already BEYOND

Suspended in time and space
Between synapses
Freed of the binds of biological limitations
We can see
We can sense
We can know
That we can
BE

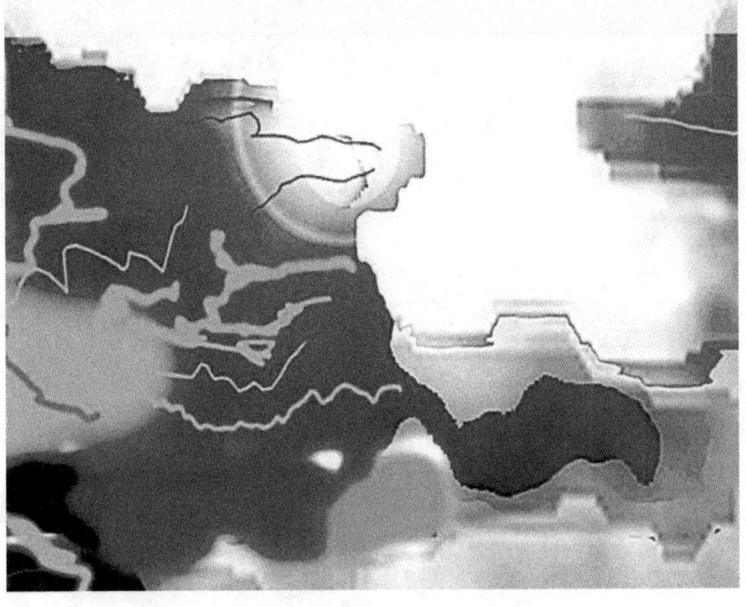

Expansion, Elevation, Transmigration:
Survival Here And Beyond: Practices And Concepts

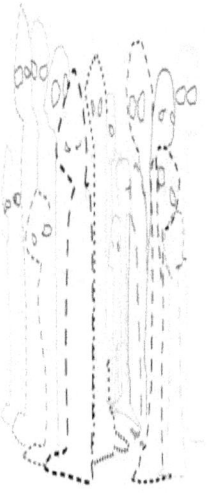

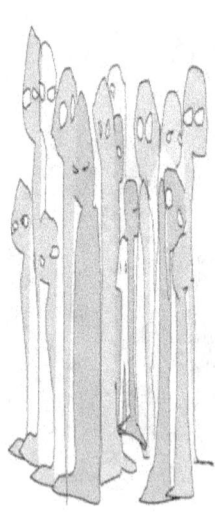

KEYS TO ACCESSING THE BEYOND

TRANSMIGRATION/ELEVATION INSTINCT: KEY #6

KNOW THE LEAP =
THE LIGHT ENERGY ACTION PROCESS

1) Of course, we know we require energy to live, to think, to feel, to work, to play. You know that every moment of your life in the physical plane, you are running your brain and body systems on energy.

2) Every signal, impulse, that LEAPS across your synapses, across the tiny gaps between nerve cells or neurons, requires an energetic event. Neurons can be said to be electrical devices. Energies in the form of ions flow, and events, such as neurotransmitter release, are triggered.

3) In this sense, all transmissions throughout our brains and bodies are energy-action processes. Ionic stimulation can result in cellular action. And the trillions of synapses in your brain are powerful transmitters. In essence, you are a powerful transmitter.

4) Allow your awareness to work with these ideas. Begin to sense (or imagine) your electrical energy, from your synaptic level on up to the whole of yourself. Imagine that you are a light generator, perhaps a light bulb beaming into space. Light is energy. Sense yourself as the light you generate and transmit.

5) For now, simply familiarize yourself with the notion of energy leaping across your synapses, and throughout the energy circuits, pathways, in your body and brain. Begin to experience yourself, identify yourself, your existence, as this LEAP itself, this <u>light energy action process</u>. Examine the possibility of being your synapses and energy pathways without your physical body. Make notes on what this imagining shows you.

Expansion, Elevation, Transmigration:
Survival Here And Beyond: Practices And Concepts

KEYS TO ACCESSING THE BEYOND

About this
TRANSMIGRATION / ELEVATION INSTINCT: KEY #6
KNOW THE LEAP =
THE LIGHT ENERGY ACTION PROCESS

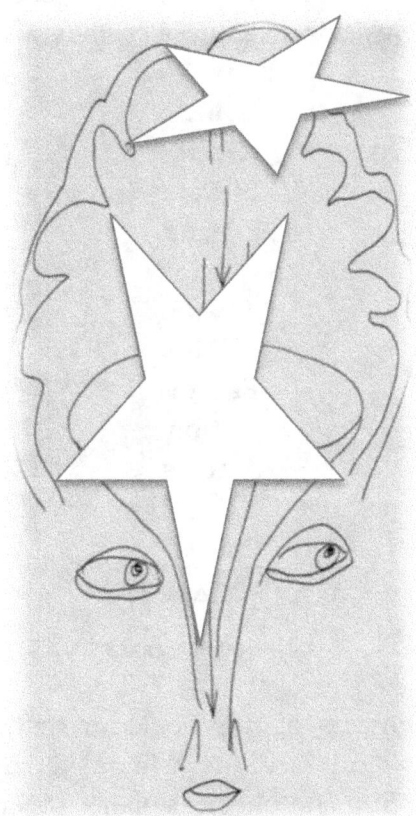

THIS PRECIOUS INSTINCT

Deep within we carry this precious instinct we are calling ourselves to (re)discover and (re)activate now. In our deepest awareness we know this TRANSMIGRATION sense and its ELEVATION capability.

<u>Expansion, Elevation, Transmigration:</u>
<u>Survival Here And Beyond: Practices And Concepts</u>

Indeed, it is our consciousness itself that knows of this, can SEE that we are able to shift focus, to LEAP into METAXIS as needed to repair injured and ailing systems, bodies, species, biospheres, or to shift ourselves, our awareness-es, to new niches....

SEE:
Shift
Elevate
Expand

LEAP:
Light
Energy
Action
Process

Into...

METAXIS
the Meta-Axis

Note: See later chapters of this book for definitions of these concepts. Here, simply see the **Meta-Axis** as a higher or transformative level of the physical plane 3-D axis (e.g., of the physical 3-D Earth globe polar axis). The Meta-Axis suggests a dimensional movement along various interdimensional axes, moving from <u>a linear 3-D dimensional continuum (a linear DC)</u> to one extending beyond the physical plane, <u>an interdimensional continuum/DC (an IDC)</u> and thus <u>an interdimensional matrix (an IDM)</u>, as described in later chapters of this book.

KEYS TO ACCESSING THE BEYOND

WE CAN CONSCIOUSLY MIGRATE

We can consciously migrate to and from one realm, one dimension or arena of reality, to another and then back again.

We Humans are already shifting and expanding. We are already seeking, identifying, <u>niches, safe niches</u>, niches beyond our biosphere on Earth, niches we can inhabit if need be.

We are doing this via what we Earth Humans call "modern space travel," yet we are also already doing this beyond the reaches of this so-called "space" travel, deep within the vast expanses of our consciousness-es.

Migration for survival by the Human Species may at some time even be migration of the mind, of the consciousness, out of physicality, transmigrating as a Species of Consciousness.

Expansion, Elevation, Transmigration:
Survival Here And Beyond: Practices And Concepts

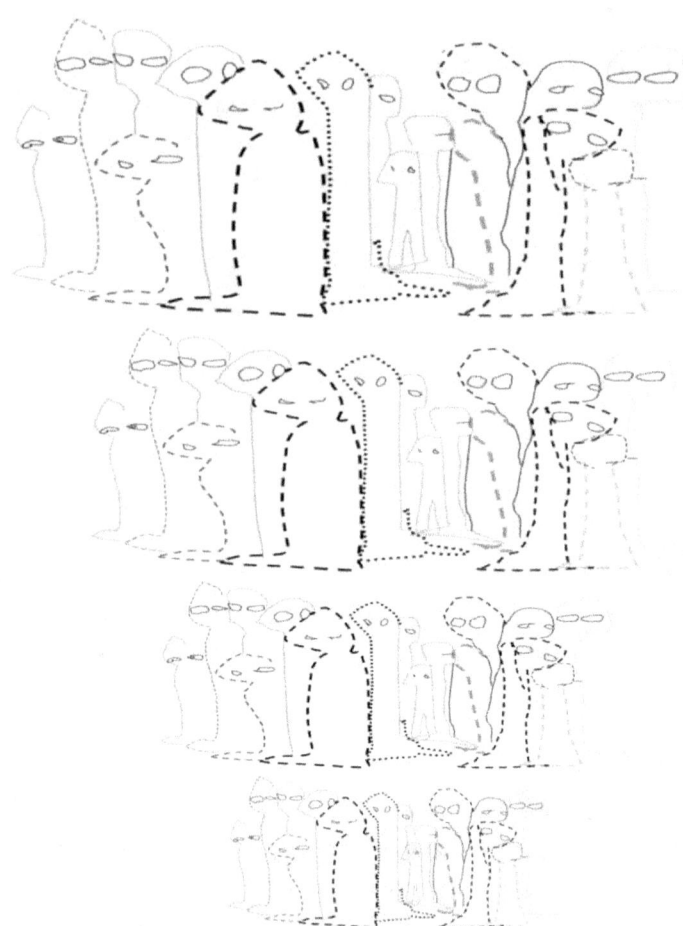

DIMENSIONS OF SELF

KEYS TO ACCESSING THE BEYOND

IMMENSE PROPORTIONS

We may not fully see this about ourselves now, at this precious point in our evolution.

Yet, it is time to recognize that we are indeed a species on an:

**evolutionary march of
immense proportions
a march across perceptions,
realities, dimensions, time …
a march of evolution …
a march for
…survival.**

We are already in the process of shifting, elevating, expanding, opening inter-dimensionally, or at least our consciousness-es are already doing so. We sense we are doing this on what we call "sub-" and "un-" conscious levels (where we are exploring this survival option).

Expansion, Elevation, Transmigration:
Survival Here And Beyond: Practices And Concepts

Responding to perceived survival pressures, our consciousness-es are seeking to prepare to adjust, adapt, transform, expand when and if needed, to shift their awareness (focus and energy) to realms, niches, where we can and do exist, including realms, niches, expansions, of our consciousness itself… <u>our</u> realms.

This awareness is more fully ours once we CONSCIOUSLY see and then <u>reach beyond</u> the constraints upon us set by the biological brain we are coded for, wired to have, that we have been "given," that we have developed or have evolved in this physical biological existence.

Note: I address the so-called sub- and un- conscious levels of all this in other books in this KEYS TO CONSCIOUSNESS AND SURVIVAL SERIES; see reading list at end of this present book. Here, let me note that what is there in these co-called sub- and un- conscious levels is there in our biological brain, but "out of our awareness" -- there where we are (our brain is) not fully consciously fully accessing it – yet.*

KEYS TO ACCESSING THE BEYOND

WE CAN REACH BEYOND

We CAN reach beyond the constraints we have either evolved into ourselves, or have arrived at by accident of nature, or that were implanted into us by designers we hardly see or understand in full.***

This is about our activating our full capacity, our rightful interdimensional awareness, allowing us to shift our center/focus, to migrate across dimensions to survive.
This access is itself (or can be itself) the next step in our evolution, if we choose this to be.

This is <u>not</u> about dying or leaving Earth per se,
this <u>is</u> about recognizing our species'
<u>full potential to consciously migrate</u>,
to shift to, even in and out of, new niches of
our minds, our consciousnesses, our realities…
         when and if needed to survive…

***Note: See reading list at the end of this present book for books in this series that discuss this matter in depth, such as OVERRIDING THE EXTINCTION SCENARIO, BOOK TWO.

Expansion, Elevation, Transmigration:
Survival Here And Beyond: Practices And Concepts

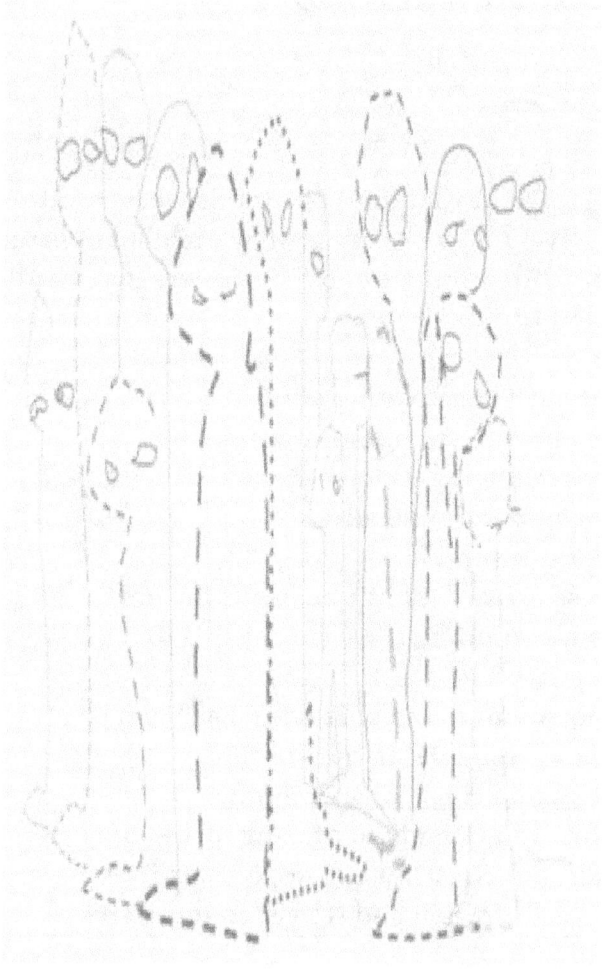

KEYS TO ACCESSING THE BEYOND

CHAPTER 7
Evolve Shift Capacity Of Consciousness To Transmigrate

KEY #7
SEE AND APPLY THE PROGRESSIVE LEAP LEVELS

αΩα

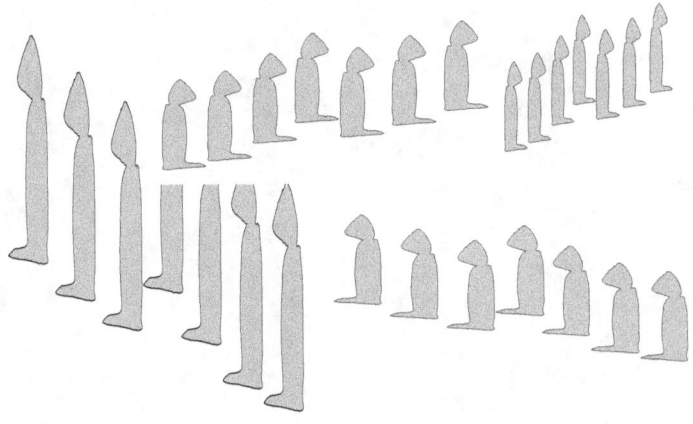

Expansion, Elevation, Transmigration:
Survival Here And Beyond: Practices And Concepts

KEYS TO ACCESSING THE BEYOND

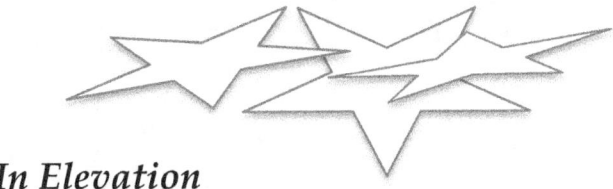

In Elevation

As you elevate, you become aware of the sensation of elevating. Recall with calm that this elevation is natural. Become this aware again.

Recall your thoughts about elevating here, your thoughts during this reading on elevating in transmigration.

Become aware that there is an awareness to experience out there, after having left the physical body. This awareness is in some instances a slow process, a slow dawning of understanding. Just wait, be there. Be in this experience, in this awareness, as it envelopes you, as it begins to bring you to itself — as you begin to bring <u>you</u> to your <u>self</u>.

This awareness is your consciousness, which has survived the leaving of your physical body. You will come to see you still exist, that who you are is not your physical body.

Expansion, Elevation, Transmigration:
Survival Here And Beyond: Practices And Concepts

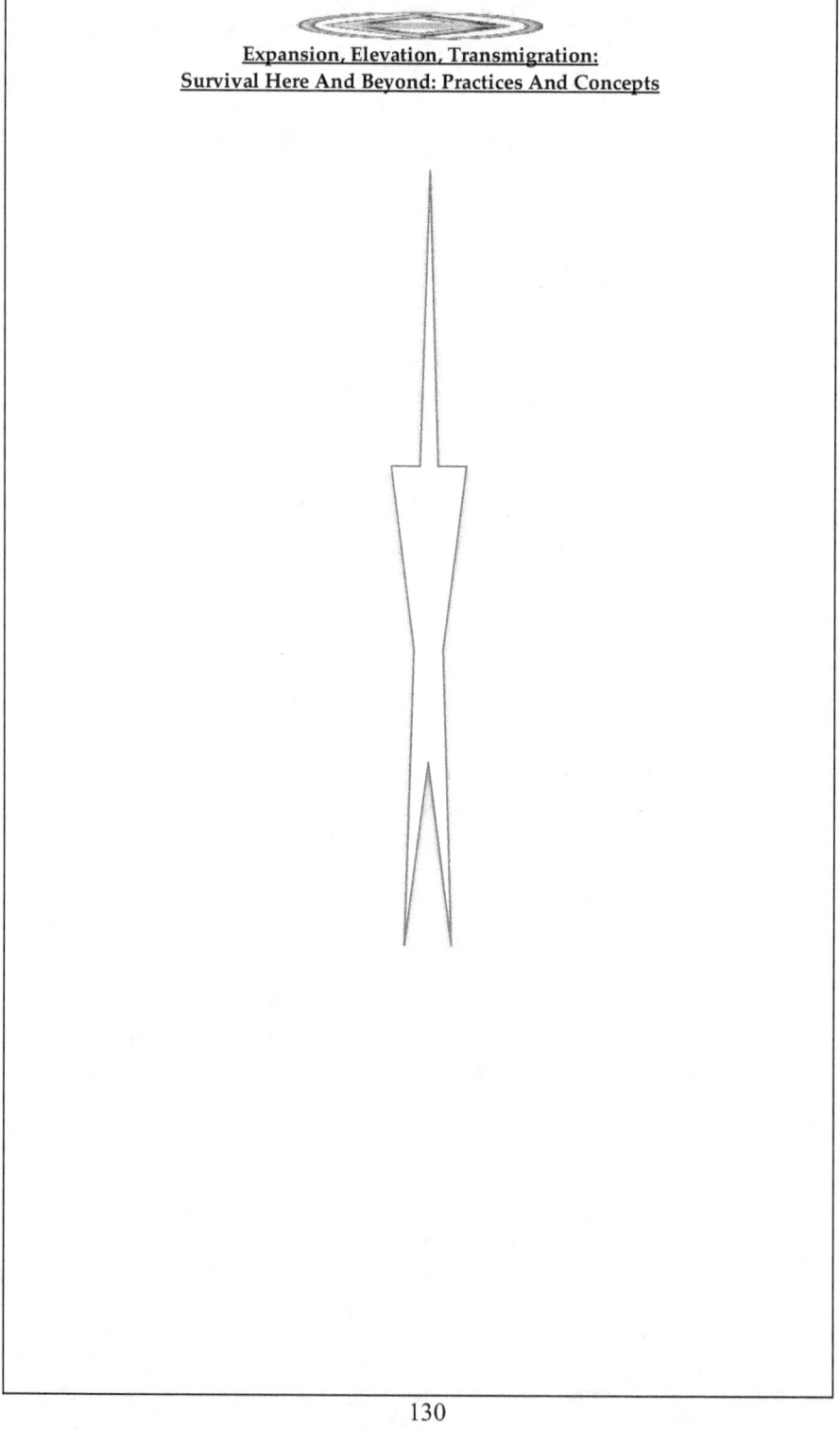

KEYS TO ACCESSING THE BEYOND

TRANSMIGRATION/ELEVATION INSTINCT: KEY #7

SEE AND APPLY THE PROGRESSIVE LEAP LEVELS

1) Living as Humans in physical, biological, bodies, we have constant, millisecond to millisecond, LEAPs taking place. Although we are generally not aware on the synaptic level of the powerful leaps taking place among our vast synaptic networks, we operate based on these.

2) We can tune into the levels of LEAP processes available to us, to the ongoing Light Energy Action Processes that we have (or can imagine we create) access to. For now, simply imagine you are aware of the tremendous movement of energy, the constant flow of messages throughout your energy pathways, including within your brain's circuitry. The synapse is one level, one form, of LEAP. Levels of LEAPs span through ranges of physicality and through non-physical interdimensional aspects of ourselves.

3) Allow yourself to imagine that there are infinite levels of LEAPs available to us, to us though our imagination functions. Imagination is a powerful means of finding this information, and or of <u>designing</u> this information and thus reality for ourselves.

4) Use your imagination to design a system of LEAPs from those tiny synapses between/among your neurons, from that micro level, on up to a macro level you imagine.

5) Now, for a moment, imagine/image moving, *leap*ing, your energy to a place in the space somewhere BEYOND your biological body and physical plane reality. Sense what this may feel like, look like, be like. Then return to your physical biological body and note what this return may feel like, be like.

Expansion, Elevation, Transmigration:
Survival Here And Beyond: Practices And Concepts

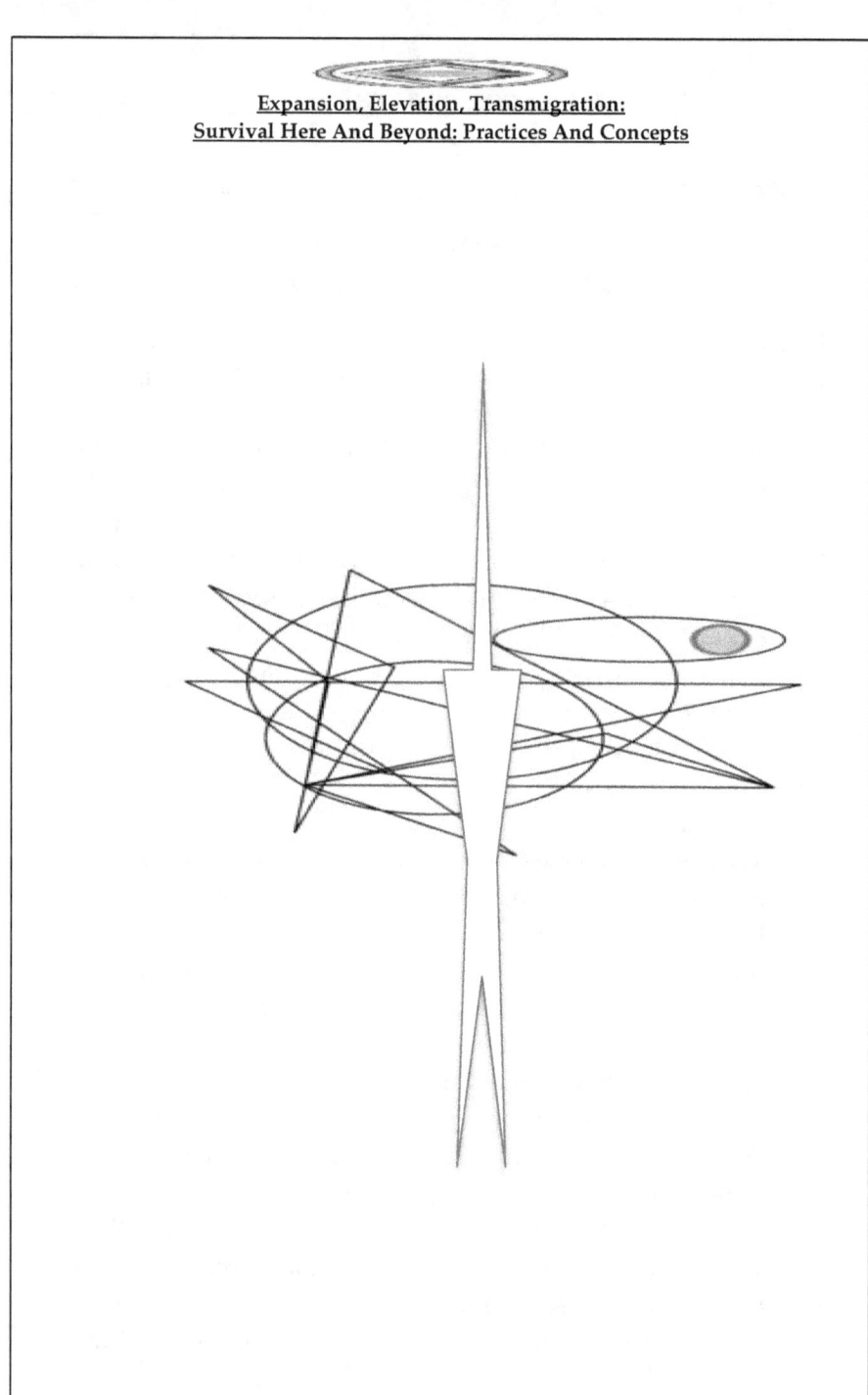

KEYS TO ACCESSING THE BEYOND

About this
<u>TRANSMIGRATION / ELEVATION INSTINCT: KEY #7</u>
SEE AND APPLY
THE PROGRESSIVE LEAP LEVELS

NOTE REGARDING THE LEAP

You can see some otherwise unavoidable physical dangers, diseases, and pollutions as possible challenges to motivate or fuel you to move out of, or in some way die out of---or let die off, a particular pattern or phase of life. This can elevate you to a new energy arrangement of your personal matrix, of your personal consciousness, of your SELF.

The LEAP defined in this KEYS TO ACCESSING THE BEYOND book (and in the related HOW TO DIE AND SURVIVE TRAININGs found in other books in this series) refers to the LEAP's LIGHT-ENERGY-ACTION-PROCESS of:

shifting the focus, the mind, the consciousness, the SELF,

from one level of awareness or reality to another.

Note: For more in-depth definition and discussion of this LEAP, see the HOW TO DIE AND SURVIVE, BOOK ONE and BOOK TWO and BOOK THREE volumes (volumes 4, 11, and 14 in this KEYS TO CONSCIOUSNESS AND SURVIVAL SERIES). See also Volume 3 in this series, UNVEILING THE HIDDEN INSTINCT.]

Expansion, Elevation, Transmigration:
Survival Here And Beyond: Practices And Concepts

Even the notion of surviving a challenge or difficult transition, even perhaps a physical death, involves a major LEAP in understanding, a rethinking of what we know or think we know about who we are and what we can do.

>This is about a LEAP in understanding,
>in knowing,
>an expansion of awareness
>at the deepest and
>most fundamental level:
>This is about our knowing
>who we actually are.

>WE DO KNOW
>WHAT WE NEED TO KNOW
>NOW.

The envelope has been opened. The energy held within the trap designed to hold us from our full interdimensional existence and identity, is freeing itself now, freeing itself for us to access within our own personal consciousness.

Note: Refer to Volume 6 in this KEYS TO CONSCIOUSNESS AND SURVIVAL SERIES, titled, OVERRIDING THE EXTINCTION SCENARIO, BOOK TWO. Refer also to other books by this author, such as those in the METATERRA CHRONICLES COLLECTION, including the novel, REVEALING THE OMEGA KEY, and the non-fiction book about all this, DETECTING THE OMEGA DECEPTION, for more on this ENVELOPE OPENING. These books explain that this is a message from us to ourselves, and from ancient elders and ascended masters and scientists, being sent to us through time.)

KEYS TO ACCESSING THE BEYOND

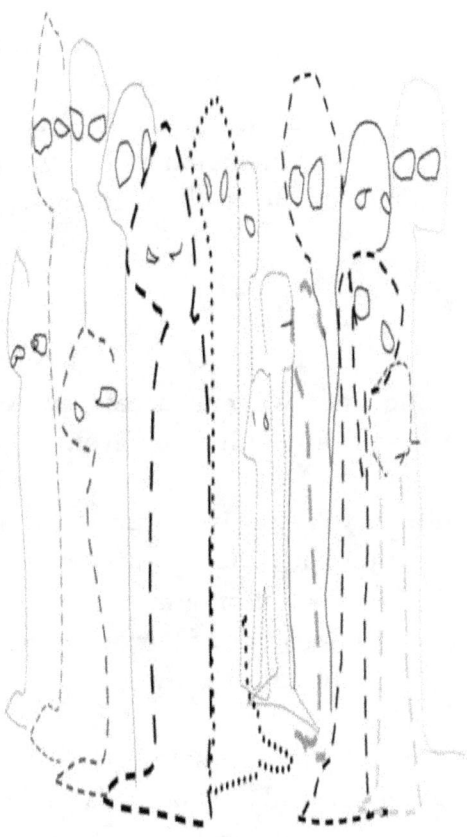

We are not a helpless species, falling prey to physical plane confusion and restriction, even fear. We are not trapped in our way of seeing ourselves, however this way evolved. We can see who we are and what we can be; we can be free to know more and be more here and beyond. As a species of consciousness, we have the capacity to work with our situation on so many levels.

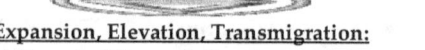

Expansion, Elevation, Transmigration:
Survival Here And Beyond: Practices And Concepts

CHANNELS

Channels in the "mind/brain" open when imagination sees into avenues not yet explored or fully open. Tools for discovery and even recovery of what we carry deep within our consciousness include our imagination, our visualization, our creative processes and activites such as drawing, playing music, and more.

THE TIME

The time may come when we must access, evolve, what we know, perceive, on a deep instinctual level:

 our species' abilities to not only migrate to safe niches here
on Earth, but to even
TRANSmigrate
across dimensions of our ourselves
and our realities

to other safe
actual and or conceptual
niches....

Note: In the non-physical niches, the consciousness elevates, transmigrates, more "fluidly" in that the tangled and dense/heavy "baggage" of physicality and its physical, emotional, and other attachment webs are not carried far beyond the physical niche.

KEYS TO ACCESSING THE BEYOND

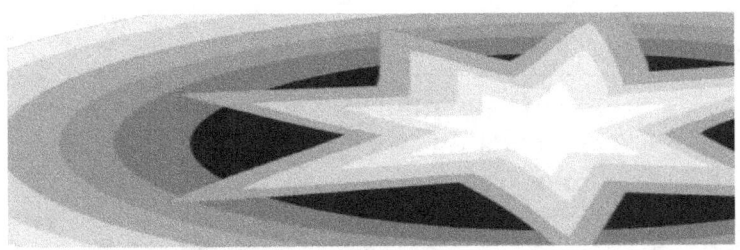

THE HUMAN MIND – AND ITS CONSCIOUSNESS – CAN NOW, AND MUST NOW,

EVOLVE ITSELF FAR FAR MORE RAPIDLY THAN DOES THE HUMAN BIOLOGY.

Expansion, Elevation, Transmigration:
Survival Here And Beyond: Practices And Concepts

THIS INSTINCT

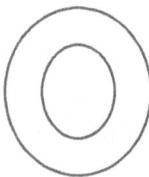

This <u>conscious shifting</u> in and out of
niches and dimensions
is something we can do,
once we
consciously know
we can do this.

Our consciousness-es already
carry this instinct,
the knowledge of
<u>migration for survival</u>,
of transmigration,
deep within us.

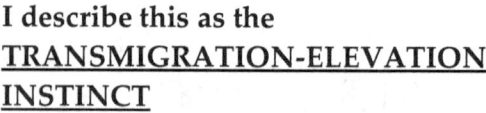

I describe this as the
<u>**TRANSMIGRATION-ELEVATION**</u>
<u>**INSTINCT**</u>
which I say is actually an extension
of the MIGRATION instinct.

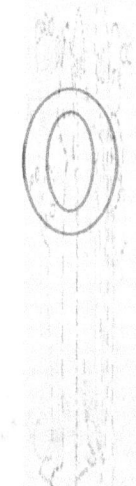

Basic physical plane Earth species'
migration across and around
this Earth biosphere
may be more obvious to us,
as we see this among
so many fellow species.

KEYS TO ACCESSING THE BEYOND

CONSCIOUS TRANSMIGRATION

However, we are also, once free to access this capability within our consciousness, capable of what I herein describe as

conscious
TRANSmigration.

Yes, we know transmigration:

We already know how to
move our energy, our focus, our matrix
across
what I define herein as the
<u>dimensional continuum</u>
(the DC)
and the <u>dimensional matrix</u>
(the DM) ...

to TRANSmigrate,
in and out of niches
and places we live
and or believe we live,
perhaps even
in and out of the physical plane
where we
ACCESS THE BEYOND.

Expansion, Elevation, Transmigration:
Survival Here And Beyond: Practices And Concepts

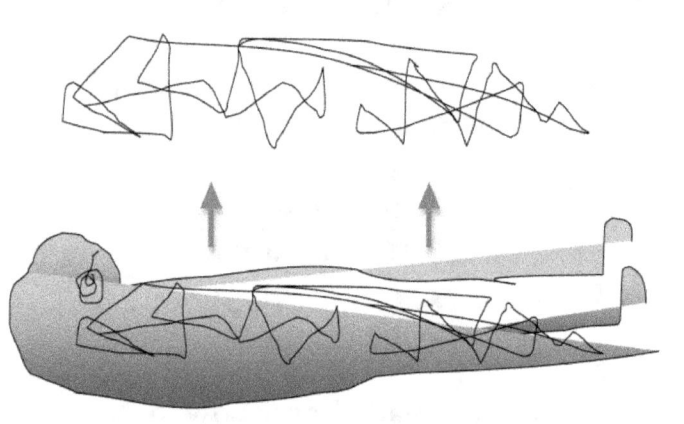

DIMENSIONAL CONTINUUM

We already live along and within a multi-directional, multi-level, non-linear dimensional continuum (DC) and dimensional matrix (DM).
We already move within
an INTERdimensional DC (IDC)
and an INTERdimensional DM (IDM).

We already move our "thoughts and minds," our consciousness-es, along, within, this infinite continuum of matrices. We come and go at will without realizing we are so doing....

Taking conscious control of this instinct, <u>this mobility awareness</u> with its <u>mobility focus/function</u> we carry within us is our right -- and may be our needed solution to eventual major personal as well as species' wide survival pressures.

KEYS TO ACCESSING THE BEYOND

We can debate
what happens when
our biological bodies die.
We can have
different beliefs about this.
We can explain the
nature of our consciousness
in varying ways.

All this is fine.
However, whatever
we believe to be the case now,
we, our species, can evolve itself
to have a say in
how we experience
what happens to us as we are born, live, and die,
or as we simply shift
in and out of physical biological form.

Just seeing ourselves as
shifting throughout the
<u>dimensional continuum</u>
<u>and dimensional matrix</u>
is going to help us know
what we need to know to survive,

and that we CAN SURVIVE.

Expansion, Elevation, Transmigration:
Survival Here And Beyond: Practices And Concepts

SURVIVAL OVERPOWERS

Once we realize we are not simply biological life forms, rather that we are the life form of the Human Consciousness, then ...

we can come to *see through* these *seeming* endings to our biological form as *seeming* deaths and even extinctions.

We can come to see that we can survive the extinction of our biological personal, species, even biosphere, vessels if we at some point need to (ACCESS -- even migrate to -- THE BEYOND).

****

Survival overpowers extinction.

SURVIVAL OVERPOWERS EXTINCTION.
SURVIVAL OVERPOWERS EXTINCTION.
SURVIVAL OVERPOWERS EXTINCTION.

The interdimensional survival awareness, this transmigration/elevation I define herein, will teach us this. And at the same time, transmigration/elevation can also teach us to:
> counter extinction trends by
> healing our personal, species,
> perhaps even biosphere, bodies.

KEYS TO ACCESSING THE BEYOND

AN EVOLVING ESSENCE

The Human Consciousness itself is an <u>evolving essence</u> with enormous unbounded potential.
The Human Consciousness can be, more and more, an expanding force of free will,
        its own free will…

      free to choose
           its paths, niches, and foci
              across dimensions.

And, in so doing the above, the Human Consciousness can also evolve within itself the power to strongly influence its own evolution as well as its life in physicality to heal the bodies …

      of individuals, the species,
      perhaps even the biosphere
      to regenerate, revive, repair
            a biological niche.

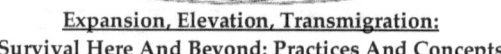

Expansion, Elevation, Transmigration:
Survival Here And Beyond: Practices And Concepts

BEING FREE STANDING

Again note: The Human Consciousness can grow more and more capable of being free standing.

Yes, this is a huge suggestion. Yet it is one that can be embraced now.

<u>The Human Consciousness
can step into itself in full --
whether it chooses to remain
traveling in biological bodies, or chooses
to shift in and out of these biological bodies,
or chooses to leave these for a time or for good.</u>

An ever more <u>free standing consciousness</u>
can know it exists with or without the
biological brain and body.
This free standing consciousness
can then shift us, move us, at will,
even rapidly,
from
state of mind to state of mind,
reality to reality,
dimension to dimension,
as needed for personal as well as species
healing, safety, survival.

KEYS TO ACCESSING THE BEYOND

Ultimately,

**our consciousness itself
is our niche....**

Expansion, Elevation, Transmigration:
Survival Here And Beyond: Practices And Concepts

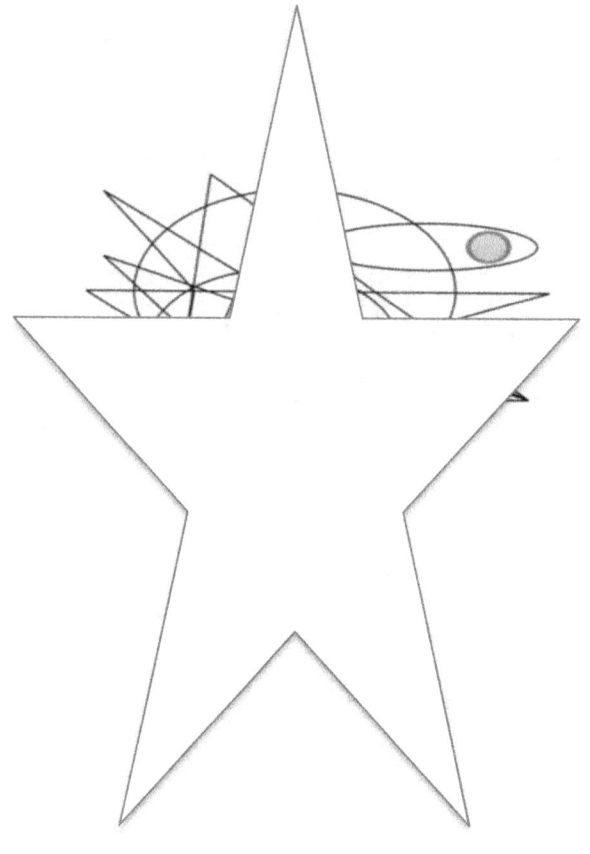

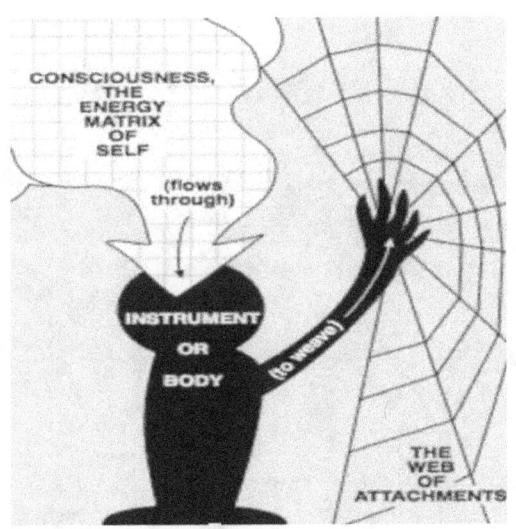

CHAPTER 8
Activate And Navigate
The Release Process

KEY #8
SEE/SENSE THE WEBS WE WEAVE
TO RELEASE FROM THEM
WHEN IT IS TIME

αΩα

Expansion, Elevation, Transmigration:
Survival Here And Beyond: Practices And Concepts

KEYS TO ACCESSING THE BEYOND

Shifting Yourself

*Of course,
shifting yourself
from one place to another
can be simple in the physical plane.
You simply find a way to go there,
a way to
walk or swim or ride or use other transportation
to the place you wish to go.*

*And shifting your awareness,
your focus, in essence your **self**,
to and from the physical plane
is also quite simple
when you have an expanded sense of
what expanded self is.*

Expansion, Elevation, Transmigration:
Survival Here And Beyond: Practices And Concepts

KEYS TO ACCESSING THE BEYOND

TRANSMIGRATION/ELEVATION INSTINCT: KEY #8

SEE/SENSE THE WEBS WE WEAVE
TO RELEASE FROM THEM WHEN IT IS TIME

1) Transmigration concepts can be valuable in working with behavioral, emotional, and physical health patterns of individuals and groups. Start with looking at this on the individual level, specifically your own. (Again, always in this work, see a physical/mental health practitioner if you are experiencing symptoms interfering with your well-being.)

2) The practice of elevating your awareness out of your body can be useful in the de-somatization and re-somatization processes referred to on these pages. *Elevating is transmigration.* Consider de-somatization a form of elevating (transmigrating) out of physicality, even if just a "short" distance out for a brief time. From outside the physical body, its physical, emotional, behavioral patterns can be scanned for, observed, amended.

3) Briefly move a short distance out of your physical body. Observe the body you are outside of. Look for what appears to be a web or ball of yarn both surrounding and within your body. At first this web or tangle will appear faint, yet after you observe for a while you will learn to better see this. For now, simply allow your imagination to help you see what is there.

4) Notice areas of this web where there appear to be knots or dense tangles, perhaps areas where you sense energy or light is trapped or not moving. For now, simply look at these areas and imagine light beginning to flow more freely through them.

5) Move back into your body. Makes notes on what you have seen and the energy you may have moved. Revisit this exercise again in the future.

Expansion, Elevation, Transmigration:
Survival Here And Beyond: Practices And Concepts

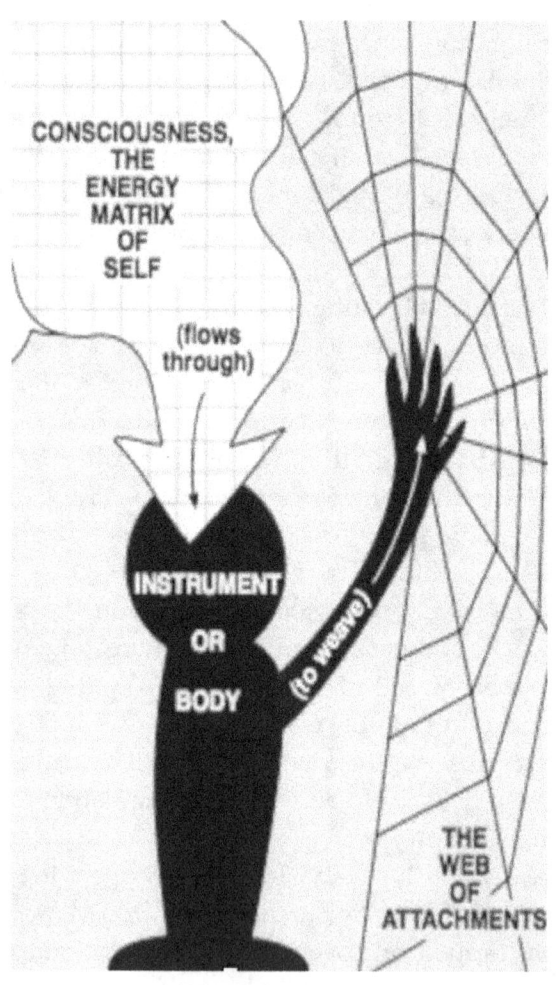

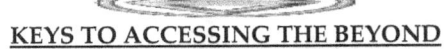
KEYS TO ACCESSING THE BEYOND

About this
TRANSMIGRATION / ELEVATION INSTINCT: KEY #8
SEE/SENSE THE WEBS WE WEAVE
TO RELEASE FROM THEM WHEN IT IS TIME

Transmigration/elevation out of physicality involves releasing the perceived and actual webs of cords and ties (attachments), and their patterns, formed by physical biological beings.

This is about, only at the right time, only at will, only when ready, only if we choose to:

our releasing our own ties, cords, and their patterns, as well as those of others connected to us.

Some of these cords, ties, and patterns support us, others may restrain us, chain us, tie us to problem patterns and situations, tie us to troubled physical conditions, even tie us to physicality when we need to heal it or even leave it.

The patterns that bind us are patterns we can form and also release at will, consciously, once we understand what this involves.

Many of these patterns tie us into,
bind us to, realities we are
not necessarily best suited for,
or that are not necessarily best to
promote our further thriving and survival.

<u>Expansion, Elevation, Transmigration:</u>
<u>Survival Here And Beyond: Practices And Concepts</u>

These patterns are like webs, cords, sometimes even chains, attaching us, even binding us, to situations and conditions we face in biological physicality.

Lifting our perspective, our angle, our point of view, rising out of these patterns to better see them, allows us to reach in and rearrange them, and or to free the energy trapped in them, <u>*to work with them from outside them.*</u>

We can know this when we perhaps may need to be able to <u>*come and go from physicality as needed to heal.*</u>

As we shift our understanding of what is going on, we start to see, sense, perceive, what we have woven as physical plane beings, the <u>webs of cords, ties, attachment patterns restricting us.</u>

We also may <u>confuse</u> these lower and more dense webs occupying our personal matrix <u>for our personal matrix itself, thus for our identity.</u> However, our actual matrix is not the patterns and webs we weave while living in physicality.

KEYS TO ACCESSING THE BEYOND

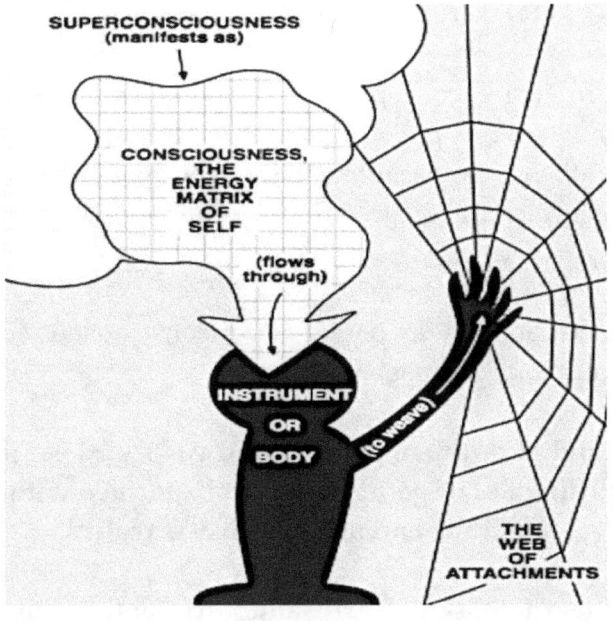

Living as biological life forms, we generate lower level emotional and biological patterns, pathways forming **webs of attachment** that tend to occupy and even confuse us regarding our actual identity, our higher matrices. Many of these patterns and their pathways and webs are quite valuable for physical survival and even convenience purposes. However, many of these patterns and their webs are confining, problematic, even dangerous. <u>Being able to shift ourselves, our awareness-es, out of these patterns and the webs they form</u> can be useful in life, in learning, in healing, in changing behavior (and perception) patterns when these are not positive for us – <u>and can also be useful as we seek to ACCESS WHAT LIES BEYOND this current LIFE.</u>

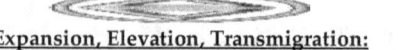

Expansion, Elevation, Transmigration:
Survival Here And Beyond: Practices And Concepts

MOVING OUT OF PATTERNS

Webs, cords, are conceptual and actual entanglements we weave to live in this physical plane. While many webs and the attachments they house are necessary for living here, these can become complex traps rather than life-helping. Stay alert to the difference.

Once we understand the power of our consciousness, we are able to consciously engage in:

**shifting out of problem patterns and webs of these patterns;
shifting out of patterns and webs formed within
and thus entangled with 3-D reality.**

We can learn to see clearly and differentiate among our various 3-D based patterns, electing which patterns to preserve and or to heal – and which to release.

This consciousness of ours is a vast and magnificent presence within us. Indeed, our consciousness IS us.

KEYS TO ACCESSING THE BEYOND

<u>We can come to know more about our own personal consciousness by bringing it into conscious focus, into heightened awareness, and by applying it to our lives, even to our survival matters.</u>

CONSCIOUSLY OVERRIDE

We can <u>consciously override</u> being controlled by the confining webs we weave, those patterns we manifest through our biological vessels. When our 3-D based patterns become problem patterns or even dangerous patterns tying us to the more difficult of our 3-D attachments and identities, we can see or amend or even expel these from ourselves so that we can be who we truly are and know this.

We can override the control of the confining webs we weave, those patterns we manifest through our biological vessels, those patterns that can chain us.

Note: For more on these webs and patterns, and the problem behaviors and addictions that these can tie us to, refer to the reading list at end of this book, specifically the book, *SEEING THE HIDDEN FACE OF ADDICTION*.

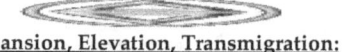

Expansion, Elevation, Transmigration:
Survival Here And Beyond: Practices And Concepts

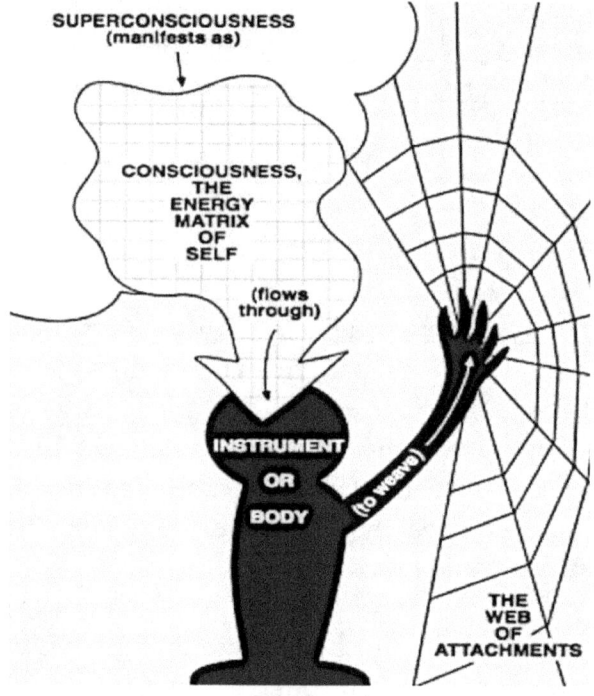

Many religious and spiritual views tell us that the individual consciousness "descends" into us from a "higher" consciousness beyond us, a super consciousness.

However the Reader views this explanation, I am suggesting that our Human Consciousness itself can assume more involvement in this relationship to its own and to other and perhaps "higher" consciousness-es, and thereby learn to relate further to its own consciousness, toward our ...

<u>consciously assuming more</u>
<u>conscious control of our own evolution</u>.

KEYS TO ACCESSING THE BEYOND

UNDER DIRECTION

Under direction of our brain, we are at all times generating, reinforcing, and living, moving, believing in, the patterns and webs we weave, confusing our physical plane based patterns and webs for our identity.
Yet, each of us knows
on a deeply conscious level that
who we are is our personal matrix.

****

Under control of our brain...we tend to be <u>so attached</u> to the set or web of our neutral, positive, and negative patterns, for example so attached to the habits, addictions, behaviors, and beliefs we form while biological beings, that we come to <u>feel</u> that this web is central to our identity, is the extent of our identity --- <u>although we generally do not realize we are doing</u> this *reduction of our identity, of our self definition*. Our brain creates and maintains this definition and <u>reduction of our identity for us, to control us</u>.

****

Once we understand that our full matrix is who we are, that this matrix is far more than the most obvious lower level web of <u>biologically based and developed</u> patterns (e.g., patterns of behavior and attachment) we weave while living in biological bodies with biological brains, then we can begin to understand that ...

   our personal non-physical matrix is our actual identity

far more than is a lower level web of most obvious physical plane formed patterns.

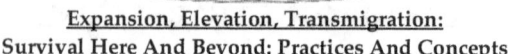
Expansion, Elevation, Transmigration:
Survival Here And Beyond: Practices And Concepts

We can see where we may be
pulling, absorbing, the problem patterns of others
into our own physicality and vice versa.
For example, we can bring
others' stress into flesh
such as into stress related
physical
disease.
We can call this <u>shared somatization</u>
or even <u>transfer somatization</u>.

I suggest that this
somatization can also be
shifted out of, DEsomatized,
once we understand that
we can readily <u>shift
our focus and energy
in and out of our physicality</u>.
Thus, as we can somatize,
we can also
<u>DE</u>somatize
the patterns we have taken on,
and do so by lifting our focus,
even our entire matrix,
out of our physical body.
Indeed, it is this interdimensional
survival awareness that may even someday
override our biological extinction.*

Note: See *Volume 5* in this *KEYS TO CONSCIOUSNESS AND SURVIVAL SERIES*, titled
OVERRIDING THE EXTINCTION SCENARIO, Part I.

KEYS TO ACCESSING THE BEYOND

SOMATIZING IS DIMENSIONAL: DIAGRAM

THE PROCESS OF SOMATICIZATION OF OUR OWN AND OTHER PERSON'S ATTACHMENTS MAY PULL OTHERWISE RELATIVELY NON-PHYSICAL PATTERNS FROM THE LOWER WEBS INTO PHYSICALITY

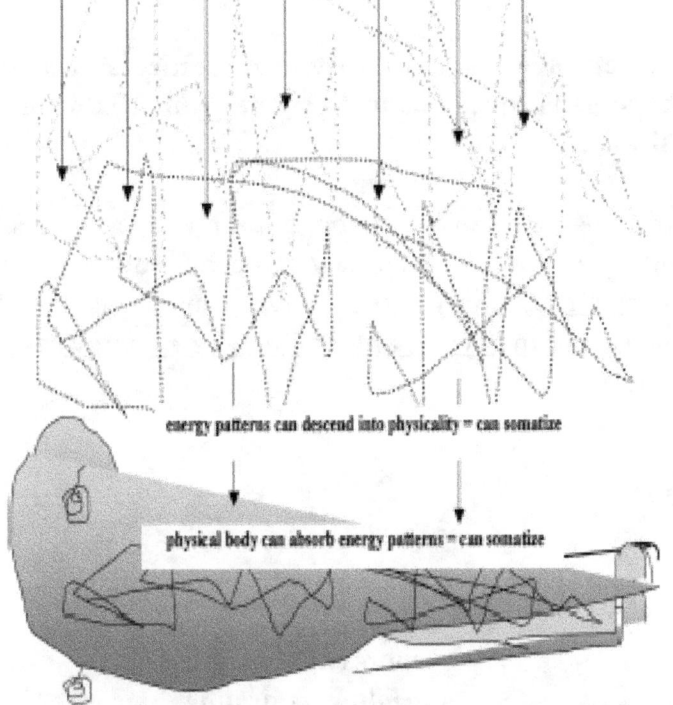

energy patterns can descend into physicality = can somatize

physical body can absorb energy patterns = can somatize

THE ALTERNATIVE PROCESS OF DE-SOMATICIZATION CAN FACILITATE HEALING

RELEASE FROM SOMATIZING IS DE-SOMATIZING

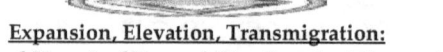

Expansion, Elevation, Transmigration:
Survival Here And Beyond: Practices And Concepts

SOMATIZING AND DE-SOMATIZING

Ever more consciously seeing these processes of:
SOMAtization and DE-somatization
can be an empowering advance for the individual Human and thus for the Human Species.

It is in our species' capability to recognize and to shift the awareness, its consciousness, its energy matrix, in and out of physicality.

In so doing, we can be seeing more about our physical and biological webs and systems, even reaching down into these -- to be <u>rewiring</u> our physical selves, amending and healing physicality <u>from beyond physicality where energy can be more fluid</u> ...

*more capable of
amending, reforming,
shifting,
even physical problem
patterns and conditions.*

KEYS TO ACCESSING THE BEYOND

*In our species consciousness lives our ability to ...
collectively "work" with streams, directions, arrangements,
and flows of energy affecting our physical and our non-physical
bodies and systems.*

There is tremendous potential
embedded within our own
consciousness' capability
to "do" this "work."

Moving a problematic
situation out of physicality
to redirect it, to reweave it, to rewire it,
can facilitate a change or shift out of
a problem web of troubled patterns.

We can heal or simply release
patterns that have occupied
the webs we as physical beings have woven,
to free our own and our SPECIES MATRIX
of the problem patterns and troubled webs
biological bodies and beings in them can weave.

**We can bring into the <u>conscious awareness</u> of ourselves
and of our species the as yet untapped actual power of
our collective consciousness.**

Expansion, Elevation, Transmigration:
Survival Here And Beyond: Practices And Concepts

KEYS TO ACCESSING THE BEYOND

CHAPTER 9
Know Our Species May Choose To Shift To Survive

KEY #9
DEVELOP/ENHANCE OUR CONTINUUM MOBILITY AWARENESS

αΩα

Expansion, Elevation, Transmigration:
Survival Here And Beyond: Practices And Concepts

KEYS TO ACCESSING THE BEYOND

Not Way Out Here Alone

We are not way out here alone; we are not an isolated island of being. We are not the only collection of conscious, even intelligent, energy, of relatively or highly conscious matrices of consciousness out there or in here....

Transmigration out of physical form can be a profound, even at times disconcerting, experience. Where at first there may be a sense of floating within an overwhelming immensity, thereafter there may be a sense of oneself (whatever that "self" is at this point) being of overwhelmingly miniscule smallness within that immensity. That sense may arrive with a vague "loneliness" in what at first may appear, seem, compute, to be a vast uninhabited cosmos....

If you find yourself in this sense, just be there. Stay present. Simply be, exist in that moment, regaining awareness, coalescing a conscious awareness, an awareness of this awareness....You will very soon be at home in all this.

Blink and here you are. Welcome home again.

Expansion, Elevation, Transmigration:
Survival Here And Beyond: Practices And Concepts

KEYS TO ACCESSING THE BEYOND

TRANSMIGRATION ELEVATION INSTINCT: KEY #9

DEVELOP/ENHANCE OUR
CONTINUUM MOBILITY AWARENESS

1) We are already moving along several dimensional continuums (continua). Every moment, we move along and within the three dimensions we "know" to be our 3-D physical reality: length, width, depth. We are also moving through other dimensions such as time, known as the fourth dimension, for example as we drive across town, fly around the world, even age.

2) Invite yourself to sense and recognize <u>your presence</u> within as many dimensional continua as you like. Imagination is, as usual, quite valuable here. Take a few minutes to do this.

3) Become **aware** of yourself in this physical plane, in this body you travel in, your physical body. Sense yourself being located within your body. Be aware of your awareness of your location.

4) *Imagine* that you slowly lift, just a "little bit," outside your body. *Imagine* you are "above" or "next to" your body. Be aware of yourself there, just a little outside your body.

5) This <u>sensing yourself</u> may or may not be easy to do, let alone to describe to yourself or others. You may or may not have precise words to describe this <u>subtle awareness</u> to others, or even to yourself. You will become increasingly familiar with this state of being, with who you are. Whether you are with or without your physical body, if you are in some way <u>aware you are there, then there you are (this "there" being where you "feel" you are).</u>

6) Now, once you are with yourself "out there," just a little outside your body, imagine you move yourself a little further beyond. Go a distance you sense you are able to move or travel, or be in. How do you do this? What do you sense there?

7) Move back, return, into your physical body. Always make a point of purposefully doing this return as long as you live in your physical body. You can return your awareness, your focus, to the beyond body sensation/state (BBS/S) again and again. You can get to know more about yourself "out there" while still living "here."

Expansion, Elevation, Transmigration:
Survival Here And Beyond: Practices And Concepts

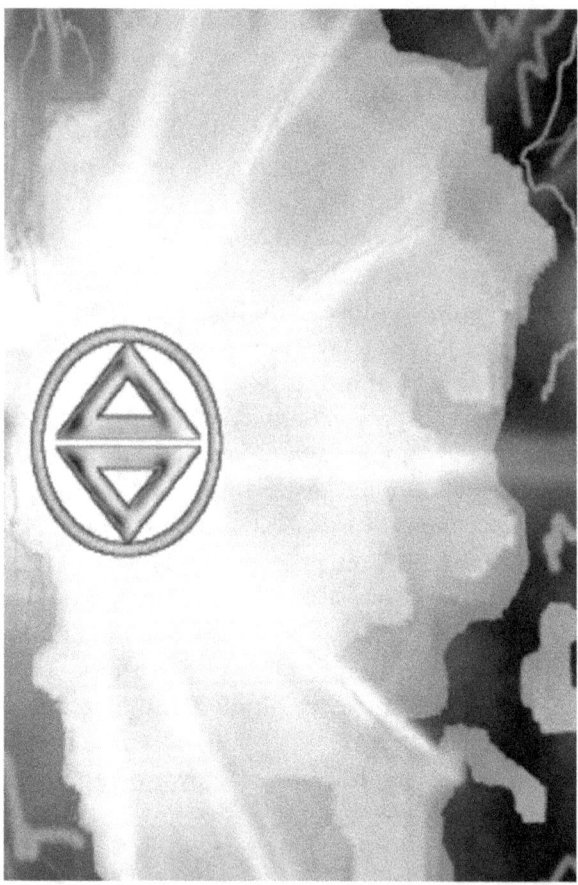

KEYS TO ACCESSING THE BEYOND

About This
TRANSMIGRATION / ELEVATION INSTINCT: KEY #9
DEVELOP/ENHANCE OUR
CONTINUUM MOBILITY AWARENESS

We can become increasingly sensitized to the unseen, the subtle, sensations and developments in the non-physical atmosphere around us. This place is not really new to us, as we are already immersed in this atmosphere. This is where we already do live, even when we live here in the material plane in our biological bodies. As we see more and more of our non-physical reality, we understand we already do live both in our physical plane reality, and BEYOND. <u>Therefore, elevating or lifting out of physicality is more a state of mind than a change in our actual location.</u>

ELEVATING OUT OF PHYSICALITY

As you are elevating (your SELF, your awareness) out of physicality, you can gain perspective. Look "down" into the density of your physicality, of your physical body, and "see" the patterns and webs you weave. See these webs throughout and surrounding you, tying you up. <u>Know that:</u>
<u>you are not these webs, not these patterns.</u>

When we see reality this way, we can then see that <u>our biologically based patterns are not our identity</u>. We can also begin to shift away from identifying with the physical vessel, biological body, we inhabit, as this is not our identity, it is our vehicle.

Expansion, Elevation, Transmigration:
Survival Here And Beyond: Practices And Concepts

As we begin to further embrace, identify with, the non-physically based aspects of ourselves, we begin to understand how mobile we are:

<u>we sense our actual mobility,
our inter-dimensional mobility.</u>

Our consciousness can know,
express, direct,
BE, this mobility.

We can understand how
fluid and flexible
our awareness,
our presence,
our locus (location),
our focus (and focal point)
our existence itself, is.

KEYS TO ACCESSING THE BEYOND

DE-SOMATIZING

Moving (or elevating) out of the biological body is what I define as transmigration, even as DE-somatization.

As is transmigration/elevation itself, <u>DEsomatization</u> is primarily conceptual, utilizing imagination functions to guide the shifting of focus,
of energy, of awareness --
out of the soma, out of the
physical body,
out of physicality and out of
<u>physicalized</u> patterns, out of
webs of attachment that weigh down, occupy, the personal (or species when on the species level) matrix.

<u>Conceptual DEsomatization</u> can guide itself to reach past the individual matrix to the species level matrix.

Species DEsomatization capability may be useful where our species as a whole may need to apply our collective species consciousness in order to group elevate or group DEsomatize, at least temporarily, to:

- LEAP

  - SHIFT

    - TRANSMIGRATE

…our energy networks, our matrices themselves, to heal them or to move them to safe niches, to realms we can visit or inhabit to survive.

Expansion, Elevation, Transmigration:
Survival Here And Beyond: Practices And Concepts

Know that these realms I speak of here are expanses, niches, of our realities, of our consciousness-es. These niches can be (as we living on Earth "know" these) physical and biological, yet can also be (or reach) outside the physical plane.

So, these can be niches in the physical world around us, or niches in our "minds," in the realms of our consciousness-es, which are ultimately one in the same.

Ultimately, our consciousness-es can show us that there are only <u>conceptual boundaries</u> between what we Humans call "internal" and "external."

We can and may at some point wish or even need to ...
<u>shift</u> our focus to, or in and out of,

        new realms
            for healing, seeing,
                even survival purposes.

Note: As I explain in other books in this KEYS TO CONSCIOUSNESS AND SURVIVAL SERIES, this shift is *migration*, and when this migration is a shift across dimensions of reality, this is <u>TRANS</u>migration. Species wide <u>dimensional expansion</u> or shifting, elevating, is species TRANSmigration. Just as we as individuals can learn to at will DEsomatize, to TRANSmigrate our focus/foci, our "selves," from, and to and from, and in and out of, a particular *physicalized body or pattern*, we as a species can learn to do this as well.

KEYS TO ACCESSING THE BEYOND

This simple concept is actually simple once we see how readily we intuitively know this. ... as we can quite easily be shifting our awareness, the <u>center of our focus –</u>
and see how this shifting of awareness and focus shifts us.

Indeed, we are shifting our focus (F) and focus energy (FE) thus our focal point (FP) all the time, almost moment to moment, without realizing what this says about what we can be and do.

As a species of consciousness, we are doing this species-level focus shifting (FS), shifting our species focus energy (FE) and species focal point (FP) on an ongoing basis. Both as individual personal matrices (PMs) and as species matrices (SpMs), we are our <u>energetic CENTERS of focus and awareness</u>.

Shifting these CENTERS shifts us as individuals <u>and as a species</u>
<u>when a critical mass</u>
<u>of the species</u>
<u>is consciously</u>
<u>involved</u>.

<u>Shifting the awareness out of the physical plane can in essence be a DEsomatization</u>, as this is lifting the awareness, the focus, of the matrix (of the individual and or of the species) out of its physical body or bodies to allow it to rewire, rearrange, revive, repair, to heal its physicality, or to shift to new places.

An entire population or species may indeed DEsomatize together, to shift its population or species <u>awareness, its center of focus, its matrix</u>, if the need is great enough.

Expansion, Elevation, Transmigration:
Survival Here And Beyond: Practices And Concepts

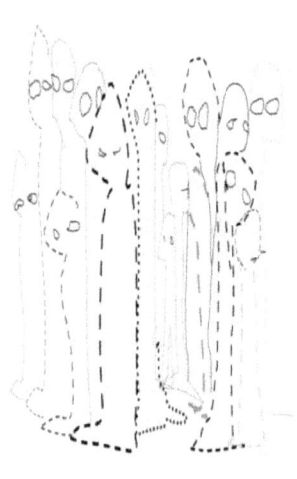

elevating
population
or
species
matrices

 ← ← DIMENSIONAL CONTINUUM → →

KEYS TO ACCESSING THE BEYOND

↑ ↑ DIMENSIONAL CONTINUUM ↓ ↓

And there may
even be a time
when
we, as a species,
or in connection
with
other species
in our biosphere,
may choose to shift the
<u>dimensional center</u> (DC) of ourselves,
or of our group of species,
even of our niche, of our biosphere itself.

**This can be a
transmigration/elevation
of the niche, even of the biosphere itself.**

Expansion, Elevation, Transmigration:
Survival Here And Beyond: Practices And Concepts

**Elevating the
planetary biosphere
is <u>mass transmigration</u>
(but not necessarily the
transmigration of its mass).**

KEYS TO ACCESSING THE BEYOND

States of "mind" can shift
as can
other forms and formats,
matrices,
of existence.

When we think of
ourselves
shifting dimensions,
this is as
conceptual as actual,
as this is a process
navigated by our
consciousness,
our
individual consciousness-es, yes,
and also our species consciousness.

Elevating is
rising to new
conceptualizations
of our reality,
of who we are,
of our identity,
and is
already moving along
this vast
(inter)dimensional matrix continuum
where we
actually do live.

← DIMENSIONAL CONTINUUM →

Expansion, Elevation, Transmigration:
Survival Here And Beyond: Practices And Concepts

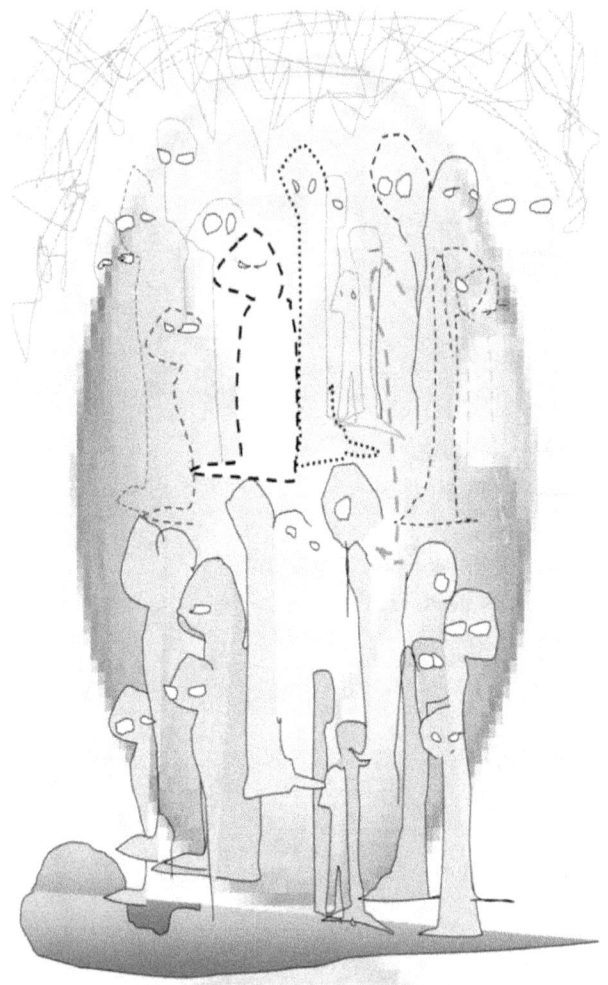

← ← DIMENSIONAL CONTINUUM → →

BIOSPHERE ELEVATING

KEYS TO ACCESSING THE BEYOND

We lifeforms can be consciously
elevating in unison, conjointly,
our
individual,
population/species,
and planetary ecosystem,
awareness-es, matrices ....

As per my definition of
transmigration-elevation,
I am suggesting that this
<u>transmigration-elevation is an instinct</u>,
an instinct we have lost touch with
or somehow been blocked from
knowing we carry.

We can begin to understand
transmigration-elevation is
instinct
just as is the
seasonal and other migration,
perhaps even immigration,
we see fellow
beings and species
on Earth engaging in:

INSTINCT.

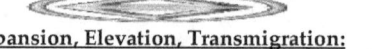

Expansion, Elevation, Transmigration:
Survival Here And Beyond: Practices And Concepts

Of course
it makes sense that
we living species have instincts
to move or migrate away…

from less food to more food,
from a climate that is
too harsh for us
to one we can more easily endure,
and of course
from danger to safety,
from threats to our survival
to
places where these
threats are fewer or
are absent.

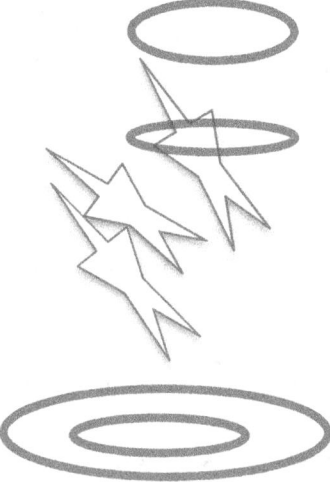

We migrate, yes,
and we
can also TRANSmigrate,
ELEVATE as our
awareness, focus,
consciousness,
to new niches.

KEYS TO ACCESSING THE BEYOND

After all,

we are all in on this survival process together.

Expansion, Elevation, Transmigration:
Survival Here And Beyond: Practices And Concepts

EARTH REALMS

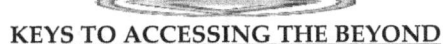
KEYS TO ACCESSING THE BEYOND

We can
learn so much
watching ourselves
and
other species
living on Earth
as biological
life forms.

Yes, the physical plane
is a great school,
much like a bicycle
with training wheels.
Among the many things
we can learn is to
consciously
move through
time and space.

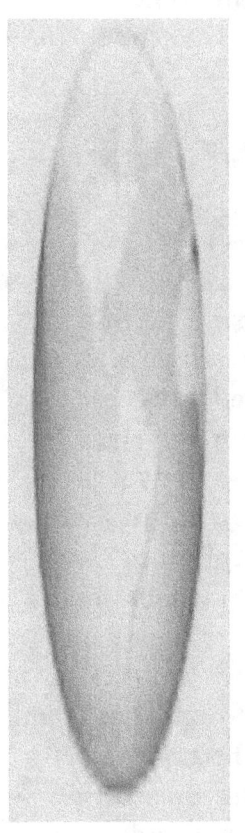

We do this moving
here on Earth every day.
We walk down the street,
drive across town,
fly over seas,
take a rocket to the moon…

and we migrate.

Expansion, Elevation, Transmigration:
Survival Here And Beyond: Practices And Concepts

We do know
what we need to know.

We can find this
knowledge
buried so deeply
within ourselves,
within our species,
within our individual
and collective
consciousness-es.

We carry within us the
vast and magnificent
depths and expanses
of our consciousness-es,
the tools and technologies
we need to migrate, yes, and
to survive, even to transmigrate:
this is
our interdimensional survival instinct.

KEYS TO ACCESSING THE BEYOND

WE CAN BE CONSCIOUSLY…
<u>navigating the transitions</u>
our species experiences
and perhaps
<u>those it senses are coming</u>,
including minor and major
predictable and also less
predictable
transitions.

We can be consciously
reading the
signals and signs
of what is coming and
of how we can prepare –

signs
in the environment –
in the atmosphere,
in the air,
in our bodies,
     in our consciousness-es.

Expansion, Elevation, Transmigration:
Survival Here And Beyond: Practices And Concepts

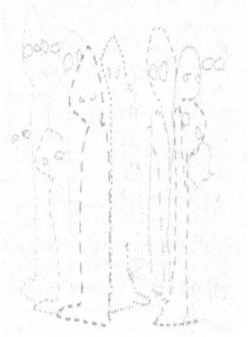

Species awareness can be
key in species survival,
our survival.
Understanding
we individual Humans
are part of <u>larger organisms</u>,
part of a species,
an ecosystem,
a biosphere,
allows us to access
key awareness-es.
We can detect extinction
possibilities.
Such awareness can sense when to
trigger migration and perhaps even
      TRANSmigration.

Note: The consciousness' awareness can sense the time for (and trigger/activate) the transmigration and its elevation. What transmigrates is not the physical (material) body, not the physical species. It is our awareness, our non-physical (immaterial) essence, which is who we truly are, our consciousness and its operant awareness. This can never be forced, *as elevation does not work (does not catalyze itself) when forced.* When we transmigrate, we move at will OUR AWARENESS, OUR CONSCIOUSNESS, out of our physical vehicles, bodies, niches, by collecting ourselves (collecting our awareness at our personal and group focal point/s), then shifting.

KEYS TO ACCESSING THE BEYOND

Instinct tells us a great deal.
We sense where we are in time and space,
and also outside of it.
Our instincts are always mapping the
environments and the
**seasons, cycles, and transitions
we are living through and
seeing or sensing are coming.**

Expansion, Elevation, Transmigration:
Survival Here And Beyond: Practices And Concepts

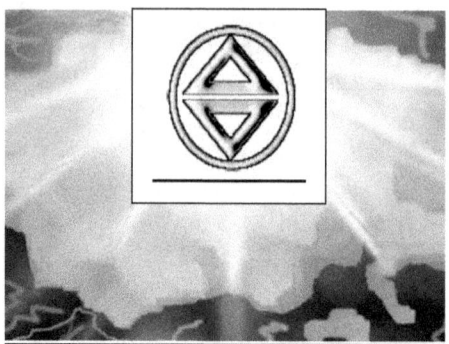

KEYS TO ACCESSING THE BEYOND

CHAPTER 10
Focus And Shift Energy To Consciously Elevate

KEY #10
FOCUS AND SHIFT ENERGY TO EXPAND, ELEVATE

αΩα

Expansion, Elevation, Transmigration:
Survival Here And Beyond: Practices And Concepts

KEYS TO ACCESSING THE BEYOND

Maintaining Focus

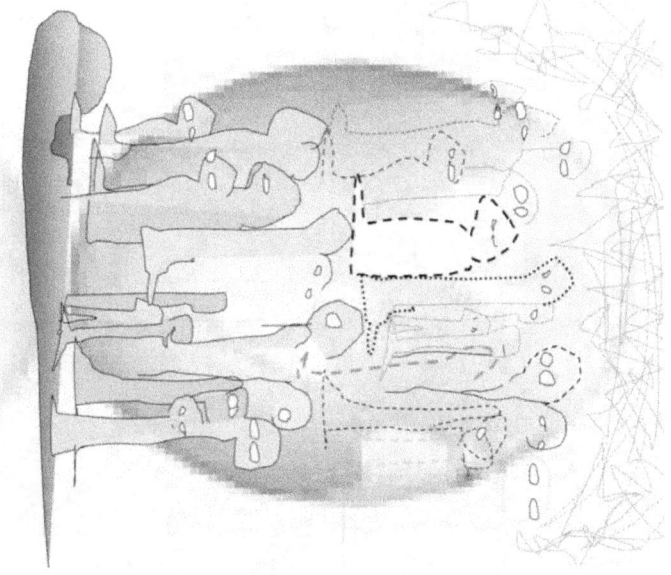

*An instantaneous full on shift, the mega-elevating, of the personal, or of the species, or even of the whole of our biosphere, into another conceptual dimension of our reality or energy is a **rush to the still racing now of time,** an expansion of such exponential proportions, so massive, that we are barely aware as it is taking place.*

No matter how instantaneous it is, there is no measure of such a LEAP in time and space, no known measure to us (none that we know we know of, that is). Yet, the consciousness we are can set itself, activate itself, to be aware and awake for this immensely profound transition, to maintain the cohesion and focus so essential in survival, so central in maintaining the conscious matrix we are and see we still can be as we survive even BEYOND.

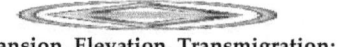

Expansion, Elevation, Transmigration:
Survival Here And Beyond: Practices And Concepts

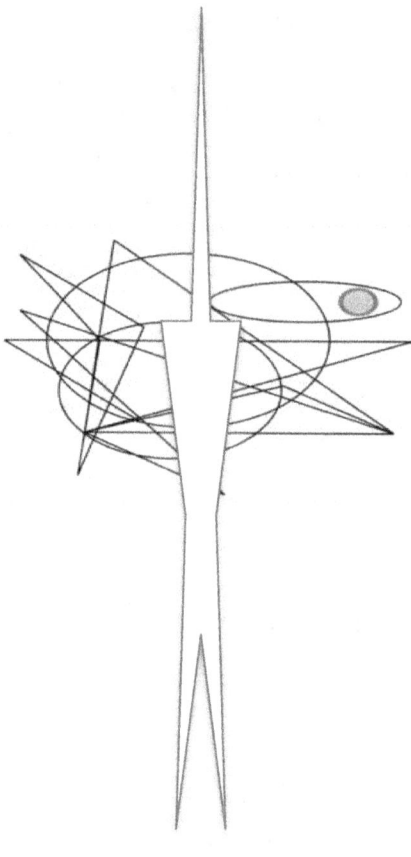

KEYS TO ACCESSING THE BEYOND

TRANSMIGRATION/ELEVATION INSTINCT: KEY #10

FOCUS AND SHIFT ENERGY TO EXPAND, ELEVATE

1) Bring the *focus of your awareness* to a single point within your physical body, such as your forehead. Pull your energy to that point. You can pull yourself to this *focal point* (FP) as this is you, the focus of your attention, of your **self**.
2) Further concentrate your SELF and your energy at your focal point. Sense (or visualize, or imagine) you are fully present at/within this single focal point, your energy collected at this focal point.
3) Slowly begin to move or shift (or visualize or imagine that you move/shift) your energy out of your physical body. We can call this <u>elevating movement</u> shifting "upward." You are elevating through dimensions as you move your focus out of physicality.
4) Continue to elevate your focal point. Move with the energy you have collected at this point. Feel yourself <u>being</u> this energy. Feel your consciousness <u>move</u> your energy, which is <u>you</u>. Do not force this process. Let your imagination and visualization guide your brain in understanding and knowing. As you practice this, simply <u>allow yourself to sense</u> you are elevating, shifting your focal point and the energy you have collected at/within this point. After several practices, you can begin to <u>SEE (shift elevate expand)</u> your focal point to nonphysical places.
5) No matter how small a "distance" you elevate (as 3-D distance is not relevant in this process), you will be learning to LEAP, which you actually do already know, hence you will be rediscovering the <u>LEAP (light energy action process).</u>
6) SEE the LEAP to focus and shift the energy you have collected to elevate, to shift your awareness which is your SELF.
7) As you elevate, realize that you are *elevating as your focal point where you have collected yourself* to transmigrate.

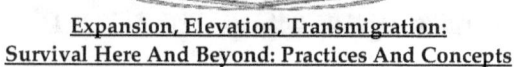
Expansion, Elevation, Transmigration:
Survival Here And Beyond: Practices And Concepts

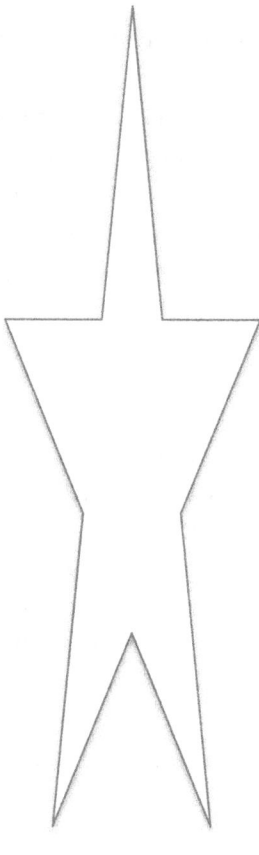

KEYS TO ACCESSING THE BEYOND

ABOUT THIS
TRANSMIGRATION / ELEVATION INSTINCT: KEY #10
FOCUS AND SHIFT ENERGY TO ELEVATE

SIMPLY MOVING, EXPANDING, THE ACTUAL SELF

Transmigration/Elevation is simply the moving of the actual SELF, of the personal consciousness, in such a manner that it <u>expands</u> along and through the

CONTINUUM OF CONSCIOUSNESS.

This expansion along and through the continuum of consciousness is itself survival.

Your continuum is your road map, your navigation plan, your expansion-elevation-ascension into what you may sense are higher frequency energy matrices, higher realms of what appears to be Light. *This non-physical continuum is where you already do live, and is where you can DIE AND SURVIVE.*

Note: This **continuum of consciousness** is further defined and described in other books in this KEYS TO CONSCIOUSNESS ANS SURVIVAL SERIES, such as Volume 10 titled, SEEING BEYOND OUR LINE OF SIGHT. See also the HOW TO DIE AND SURVIVE books, Volumes 4, 11, and 14 in this series. See reading list at the end of this present book.

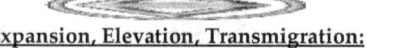

Expansion, Elevation, Transmigration:
Survival Here And Beyond: Practices And Concepts

FURTHER DEVELOPING SENSITIVITY TO THE BEYOND

We can further develop, fine tune, our sensitivity to what is not always distinctly obvious to us as we live our daily lives.

We can become ever more aware of aspects of our reality that we may not sense via our five basic biological senses. As we do so, we begin to see how essential this <u>extended sensitivity</u> is.

Part of extending our awareness can involve using the imagination functions and visual imagery processes our brain can provide us. This sort of exploration is of course creative. Imagining and visualizing are very helpful in developing awareness, as we open pathways in the brain and mind that may not be readily accessed without this practice.

Becoming more aware of things we do not see with our usual biological eyes, and do not hear with our usual biological ears, and do not feel with our usual biological skin cells, is key in extending ourselves---is key in:

expanding our concept
of ourselves and our realities
to reach BEYOND
what our minds have so far
been telling us about
ourselves and our realities.

KEYS TO ACCESSING THE BEYOND

GENERATING THE LEAP

Whether personal (individual) and or species level,
the *elevation-transmigration* we may choose to partake in
either while biologically dying or while biologically living on
(or at any other point in our existence)
is a concept, an idea,
and a state of mind, *and* a level of consciousness,
and a process
all at once.

The **shift**
of AWARENSS, of PRESENCE, of FOCUS, of LOCUS,
generates, fuels, the LEAP,
the light-energy-action-process itself.

This results in the SELF process:

SELF =
Shift-Elevate Leaps the Focus.

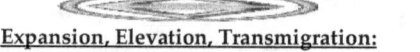

**Expansion, Elevation, Transmigration:
Survival Here And Beyond: Practices And Concepts**

**Ultimately the
mobility of the SELF
is indeed the SELF itself.**

Note: Other books in this KEYS TO CONSCIOUSNESS AND SURVIVAL SERIES define in detail this generally non-physical reality we are herein imagining, visualizing, and accessing.

Awareness of this reality is what we are further accepting and developing within ourselves in order to explore and to sensitize to---what other books in this series define and describe as---the **PATTERN TERRAIN**.

(See for example, the book, NAVIGATING LIFE'S STUFF, BOOK TWO, Volume 9 in this series.)

KEYS TO ACCESSING THE BEYOND

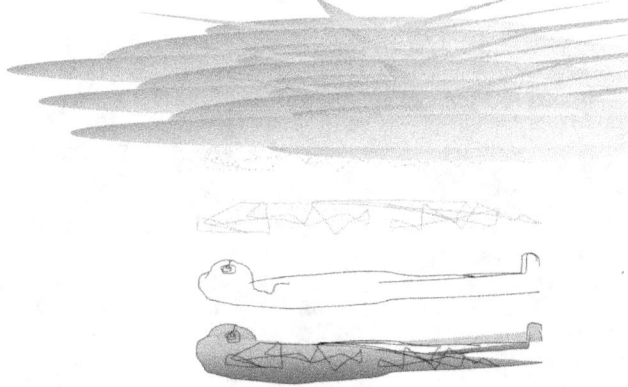

CHAPTER 11
Elevate The Individual Human Matrix

KEY #11
BEGIN TO MASTER PERSONAL ELEVATING

$\alpha\Omega\alpha$

Expansion, Elevation, Transmigration:
Survival Here And Beyond: Practices And Concepts

KEYS TO ACCESSING THE BEYOND

Next Step

There is always
A next step
Just past the end
Just beyond the place of no exit.

There is always
Hope.

Realms, new realities
Having been here all along
Await.

Such a grand undertaking
The epic journey
Calls.

Capsules of truth
Wisdom finding its way
Into our knowings.

Now time comes together
Like all roads
Leading to the same place…

Pressing the knowing
Into sight.

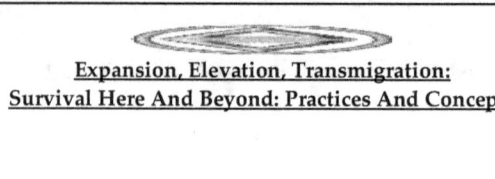
Expansion, Elevation, Transmigration:
Survival Here And Beyond: Practices And Concepts

KEYS TO ACCESSING THE BEYOND

TRANSMIGRATION/ELEVATION INSTINCT: KEY #11

BEGIN TO MASTER PERSONAL ELEVATING

1) The personal moving, shifting, DEsomatizing, *elevating* of <u>your self as your focal point, your non-physical identity</u>, is useful practice in working with problem or troubled systems, patterns, webs woven in physicality. From outside the physical plane, <u>seeing and repatterning</u> congested, confused, conflicted webs of attachment behavior and emotion can be conducted without the challenge and obscuring brought on by 3-D density and material complexity.

2) Another great value in understanding this elevating, in practicing the notion, the imagined and visualized elevation of yourself as your elevated focal point, relates to possible eventual movement to dimensions beyond physicality for temporary or permanent travel, healing, and or safety/survival.

3) As you practice elevating yourself (your focal point), take this process casually, easily. Imagine or visualize to see your awareness (with its focus and energy) moving, elevating through degrees of physicality and density. As you move beyond the physical plane, sense that physical density reduces. Feel, sense, SEE, the definite "lightening" of the environments where you are as you elevate through them.

4) Imagine or visualize you remain in that less dense environment where being a focal point of energy **is being.** Become familiar with, aware of, that reality, that place. Give it your own definition and nature. Grow comfortable with coming from and going to this place.

5) Each time you practice this, do this exploration, you must return to your physical body. This is simply a practice personal elevation to understand, grow familiar with, the concept.

Expansion, Elevation, Transmigration:
Survival Here And Beyond: Practices And Concepts

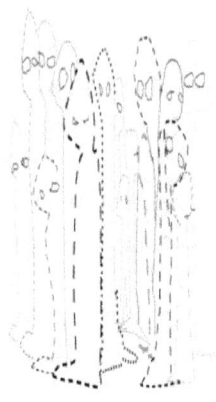

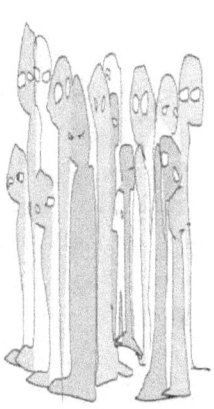

KEYS TO ACCESSING THE BEYOND

ABOUT THIS
TRANSMIGRATION / ELEVATION INSTINCT: KEY #11
BEGIN TO MASTER PERSONAL ELEVATING

For those who recall their previous out of body sensations or experiences, think of these and of how you felt when "out." Others simply imagine having these for now. Elevation is simply a word for lifting or rising or moving focus out of the physical into the energy body sensation.

TAKING OURSELVES TO NEW LEVELS
HERE AND BEYOND

All this is about how we can take ourselves to new levels of ourselves, and use this understanding in our daily in-life lives, as well as eventually in developing our end-of-life and perhaps even our after-life experiences.

Everyday we live, as we go about our daily lives, we can be expanding and elevating our understanding of ourselves and our realities. As we expand our own sense of ourselves, we can even form new views of our options in terms of survival both here and beyond, survival as who we actually already are: our own personal consciousness. (Other books in this KEYS TO CONSCIOUSNESS AND SURVIVAL SERIES have defined and discussed this matter in great depth. For example, see Volume 6, titled OVERRIDING THE EXTINCTION SCENARIO, PART TWO, and also Volume 3, titled, UNVEILING THE HIDDEN INSTINCT.)

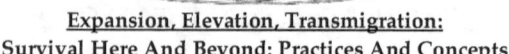

Expansion, Elevation, Transmigration:
Survival Here And Beyond: Practices And Concepts

As we further explore what it means to extend our awareness into what we can describe as other understandings, even other atmospheres, even other dimensions of our realities, we find we can use the tools we already do carry within our brains and minds.

For example, we all carry our own great resources in terms of our creativity, imagination, and visualization skills. We are constantly using these skills or functions, much of the time not realizing we are so doing.

EXTENDING INTO REALMS BEYOND

Our minds can extend us into realms beyond our everyday realities. All this leads us to new levels of what it may feel like to see beyond everyday physical plane reality.

We can apply the sense of extended awareness (or interdimensional vision) to ideas and possibilities we are exploring. While fascinating, this is not only for fun or entertainment, but also for creating working ideas and living spaces, and also for possible survival reasons.

KEYS TO ACCESSING THE BEYOND

HERE WE ARE

So here we are, each of us an individual matrix,
an individual
network of <u>energetic pathways</u>.*
This matrix is
indeed a
<u>network of energies</u>,
an energy body,
<u>a matrix of consciousness</u>.

This individual network
is the
PERSONAL MATRIX or PM.
This matrix is the
personal "energy body,"
carrying the personal consciousness.
This personal matrix is, in essence,
one's actual identity.

Note: I refer Readers to the nature of the so-called "biofield" as discussed in other books in this series, as this biofield itself is said to be a **network of energy/energetic pathways**. (See the opening chapters of Volume 3 in this series, the book titled, UNVEILING THE HIDDEN INSTINCT.)

Being somewhat aware of the so-called **energy body** we already do carry around and beyond our physical body can bring us to further knowing ourselves as non-physical beings – beings who can of course exist within, yet also perhaps independent of, our biology.

<u>Expansion, Elevation, Transmigration:</u>
<u>Survival Here And Beyond: Practices And Concepts</u>

Our coming into physicality teaches us a great deal about what it means to move within a physical dimension.

Our being *conscious* physical biological beings gives us the *opportunity to explore* what it means to have (and BE) a consciousness,
**to live in physicality with a consciousness,
and to discover what we might be able to do
as ever more conscious beings.**

**As Human Beings living on Earth,
we have come right up to the
limits of this Earthly biosphere,
of our Earth niche within this physical plane.
Our minds and bodies tell us
there may be more,
there** *has to be more,*
there is

MORE BEYOND THIS. . . .

KEYS TO ACCESSING THE BEYOND

We begin to detect ourselves, recognize ourselves, as *more than physical biological life forms.*

We detect this simply by being here on Earth and <u>exploring the limits of physicality, and yes, of life and death</u> as we know it here.

We find we are able to sense, recognize, a contrast between what we <u>can know</u> and <u>cannot know</u>, contact, of reality when coming to this contact as
physical biological beings.

**There is
far more to reality
than we generally know as
biological beings with biological brains,
with consciousness-es <u>seemingly</u> dependent upon,
tied to, our biological brains.**

Again note: As some Readers have asked whether I "recognize" the utility of psychoactive drugs or "medicines" in "exploring the mind and 'reality'," note that I do not herein debate the potential exploratory uses of some psychoactive compounds. I do however advocate for a drug free exploration of the concepts and metaphors I offer herein. My work as presented herein <u>emphasizes the understanding that</u> anything done through the biological brain, including taking "drugs and medicines," is nevertheless still being done by the biological brain. (And, I am on these pages questioning what our brain tells us, whether it be the biological brain itself or that brain "under the influence" of outside compounds/drugs).

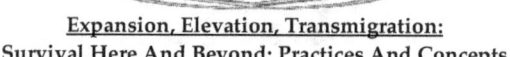

Expansion, Elevation, Transmigration:
Survival Here And Beyond: Practices And Concepts

We can know so much if we look closely, so much about the selves we have that are non-physical, <u>the selves we actually are</u>, the consciousness-es we are living with (and as) virtually every waking (and sleeping) moment of our lives.

We can see we are more than only our physicality.
Indeed, when coming into physicality,
being born here on Earth,
so much is clear to us about
who we are beyond our physicality.
We feel the contrast as we come in here.

So much is clear until the
<u>**rush of physicality**</u>
clouds our memory
of all that has been so clear.

When living here on Earth and developing here as biological Human Beings, our biological Human brains are designed to screen and select what we are *allowed to know.*

We begin to be so occupied with existence in the physical plane that our **interdimensional personal matrix**, thus our full identity, is often not obvious to us.

Instead, we more and more feel we are simply how our physical existences are defined. Our identities thus grow rather restricted, primarily to physicality and to the obvious attachment patterns and webs our physicalities weave.

KEYS TO ACCESSING THE BEYOND

EXPANSION

It is time to expand past the
restriction of
our biological brain,
to enjoy, use, and
live with this biological brain,
yet to also
reclaim our actual Human Consciousness
which can
<u>evolve itself, adapt itself,</u>
to exist independent of our biology
when it elects to ...
can move, shift to and from,
be here and beyond here.

We can learn to
move in and out of our vehicles,
including our physical bodies,
and survive,
once we understand
what it is that
CAN SURVIVE.

I thus offer these
<u>TECHNOLOGIES OF THIS SURVIVAL</u>
and these further
<u>CONCEPTS AND TECHNOLOGIES OF
TRANSMIGRATION</u>
on the following pages....

Expansion, Elevation, Transmigration:
Survival Here And Beyond: Practices And Concepts

TECHNOLOGIES OF THIS SURVIVAL

Our matrices are networks, bundles, concentrated pathways of interdimensional awareness energy.

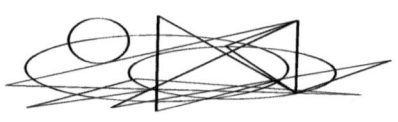

Various **networks within matrices intersect** to form characteristics of pathways and bundles of energy that can be key points of action in the LEAP, the **matrix shifting,** we may at some point want or seek to do.

Note: The model of an **energy body** surrounding the physical body includes **energy pathways** forming the **matrix** of that **non-physical body**.

KEYS TO ACCESSING THE BEYOND

BREAKING THROUGH
OUR PROGRAMMING NOT TO KNOW

We are at all times moving in, and within, and with, our individual matrix. <u>**We are actually this matrix itself**</u>. **<u>We are this matrix</u> more than we are whatever physical body we happen to occupy.** Once we understand that <u>this matrix is our identity</u>, that we are not the physical vehicle (body) we inhabit, we can understand our true mobility as our interdimensional mobility, which is our natural state.

<u>Our awareness and thus our consciousness is far more mobile</u> than is our physical body.

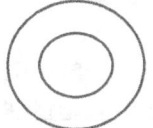

<u>**The individual matrix of you**</u> is not tied to the physical body, nor to the physical plane itself, as this matrix is not essentially physical/material.

<u>**We can see**</u> that who we are is our matrix, and that neither our vehicles (physical bodies) nor our environments (physical milieus) are who we are.

<u>**For example, if we were fish**</u> we could say that just because a fish is in water does not mean this fish is the water. (We are not our environment.)

<u>**If we were a television set picture**</u>, we could say that just because a television set brings together wires and currents to render a picture does not mean that the television set is the picture it shows: the television set is only the hardware, the vehicle, the transmitter.

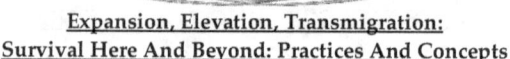

Expansion, Elevation, Transmigration:
Survival Here And Beyond: Practices And Concepts

Similarly, your biological body with its biological brain (your hardware) is not who you are.

Note again here that we are not the emotional, social, and biological webs (of attachments and the emotional and behavioral patterns around these attachments) that our biological brain builds to live in physicality, although it is <u>easy to assume</u> our webs/patterns are part of our identity, even our identity itself. <u>Our brain is wired to have us assume this.</u> Our 3-D brain determines, even requires, our 3-D identity while living in the 3-D physical body.

<u>Our consciousness lives in, IS,</u>
<u>our personal energy matrix,</u>
the energy network we have which is not necessarily tied to our physical body, which is far more our identity than the lower level webs and patterns we weave while living in a physical body. *(Even the term and concept, energy, is simply a word for something no longer real – at least in physical plane terms. Out of physicality, we sense a different form of and nature of ourselves and our energy, energy no longer entirely conceivable, definable, or measurable from a physical plane perspective.)*

This distinction between our OUT OF BODY, generally non-physical, matrix and the "lower level" webs/patterns we weave while living IN BODY, in physicality, will become increasingly clear as we proceed.

Again, terms such as "higher" and "lower" are artificial here as we are actually multidimensional matrices rather than linear.

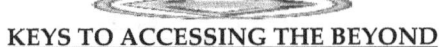
KEYS TO ACCESSING THE BEYOND

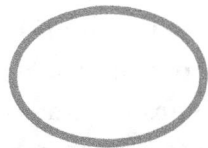

Think about this:
You are wired to think
you are your physical body,
and tied to this body.

However, you are much more mobile
than is your physical vessel.
Thinking this way, seeing you are
more than your physical biological self,
allows a more fluid and freely willed
personal mobility:

**MOBILITY OF AWARENESS,
MOBILITY OF SELF.**

In other words, you can "fly" if you wish,
just take a moment to lock the door and
leave your body home, move back into it
a moment later.
DO NOT ABANDON
YOUR PHYSICAL BODY,
RETURN TO IT TO LEARN MORE.
So, we have the option of expanding our identity
to beyond that of biological Earth Human,
expanding to include much more of who we are.

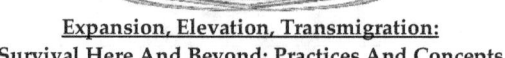

**Expansion, Elevation, Transmigration:
Survival Here And Beyond: Practices And Concepts**

Once we can detect and then expand...our biological Earth Human identity to include our more expansive identity, to be our matrix which is our actual identity-- we can heighten our ability to consciously move our focus, our center of attention, ourselves, our consciousness, in and out of physicality, in and out of this physical plane -- ever more free of control by the biological brain.

This is our advancing our
transmigration/elevation capability.

Once we accept our
transmigration/elevation capability,
accept this about ourselves,
accept that we are consciously mobile,
we can consciously
learn more about this capability
to reach across dimensions.
We can train our awareness
and thus our attention, our focus,
to come and go from physicality,
to be as expansive as we actually are.

We can consciously migrate.
We can consciously TRANSmigrate/ELEvate.
We can be consciously interdimensionally mobile.

KEYS TO ACCESSING THE BEYOND

MOBILITY CAPABILITY IS KEY TO SURVIVAL

**This is the
interdimensional shift awareness
we already carry within us.
We can come to see that
our mobility is our consciousness
and our consciousness is our mobility.**

Again note: Once out of our physicality,
we have a range of opportunities
including but not limited to:

- moving to a new or expanded
form in our present niche,
or to a new or expanded form in a new niche;

- returning to our physical form
knowing more about what this means;

- reaching from outside
our physical body
down into our own physicality,
to work on, even alter, even help,
physical and biological conditions
from outside these conditions,
acting from our own
individual energy matrix.

<u>Expansion, Elevation, Transmigration:
Survival Here And Beyond: Practices And Concepts</u>

Once we grasp how much say
we can consciously choose to have in the matter,
we can
develop ever more conscious participation in,
even direction of,
our personal and species evolution.

What I am saying here is that we are a
species of consciousness
who can choose to locate our awareness –
our attention, our focus, our center of energy,
even our identity,
where and thus as who
we wish to be, where we choose
to view ourselves as being in time and space.

**This is mobility;
this is the ability to consciously focus,
locate,
even shift.**
This <u>conscious
interdimensional
mobility</u>
is key in
the transmigration/elevation technologies
I introduce in this book
and in other books in this
KEYS TO CONSCIOUSNESS AND SURVIVAL SERIES.

KEYS TO ACCESSING THE BEYOND

This is about
consciously shifting,
elevating* *the focus of the awareness,*
in and out of physicality.
This is about what I call
personal and species shifting,
personal and species metaxis,
personal and species transmigration/elevation.

The **personal metaxis** I am defining here
takes place when the individual matrix
consciously elevates*
its awareness, focus, center of energy,
energy pathways,
out of the physical plane niche,
moving along and through the *dimensional continuum*
(DC and IDC)
and throughout the *dimensional matrix*
(DM and IDM).
This shift, elevation, metaxis,
may be temporary, or for some even permanent.
<u>We have the free will to choose, once we know this.</u>

I apply the term, *elevate,* to refer to the non-linear expansion along the non-linear dimensional continuum, which is the dimensional matrix, although elevation is diagrammed as linear herein.

Expansion, Elevation, Transmigration:
Survival Here And Beyond: Practices And Concepts

We can think in terms of the
<u>imagined or actual</u> movement,
shifting,
<u>elevation along the
(inter) dimensional continuum (IDC),
and (inter) dimensional matrix (IDM),</u>
by the person
(who is the personal matrix, the PM,
and the interdimensional personal matrix,
the IPM).
We can choose to engage in (focus within)
the interdimensional levels as needed
or desired,
knowing we actually at all times
exist interdimensionally.

Above, I say *imagined or actual*
because our way into ourselves,
into our great capabilities,
is exploratory, expansive, creative,
**bringing us access to
parts of our brain,
even to our
<u>beyond brain consciousness</u>
we may not fully access in
standard daily living
as Earth Humans.**

KEYS TO ACCESSING THE BEYOND

When we think of leaving
our physical bodies for good,
we know that we have
oft been told
to think this is "death."
However, while we are told that
this "death thing"
is what happens to us,
this may actually merely be
the physical expiration, or the retiring of,
our physical vehicle,
<u>not actual death of our being.</u>

This expiration of our vehicle (of our physical body)
need not be death,
this can be something else once we consciously understand
who we are,
that we are not a physical body that expires.

We may live in a physical body that expires, however, as we further clarify our identity, we begin to at least consider the possibility that we do not, or need not, expire …
when the
physical body does.
We can ACCESS THE BEYOND.
We can DIE AND SURVIVE.

Expansion, Elevation, Transmigration:
Survival Here And Beyond: Practices And Concepts

elevating
individual
organism
matrix

← DIMENSIONAL CONTINUUM. →

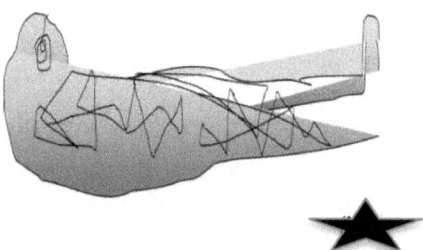

KEYS TO ACCESSING THE BEYOND

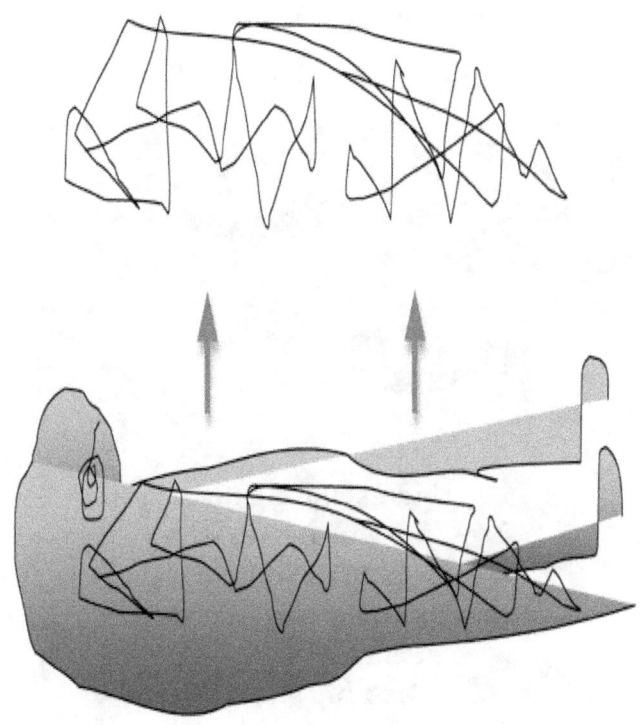

**PERSONAL METAXIS IS THE
PRIMARY TRANSMIGRATIONAL ELEVATION:
Individual Matrix
Elevating Out of Physical Plane Species/Niche
Along the Dimensional Continuum**

Expansion, Elevation, Transmigration:
Survival Here And Beyond: Practices And Concepts

SEEING
WHAT IS GOING ON HERE

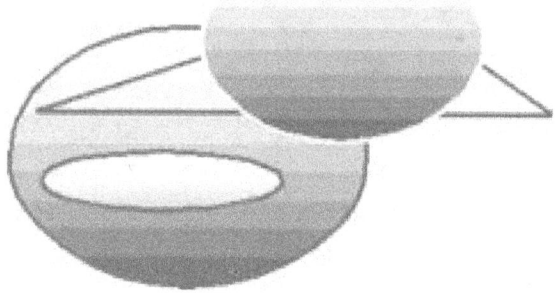

Understanding that
you are not who
your IN BODY biological brain
wants you to (is wired to)
believe you are
is a big step.

Be patient with this understanding,
as it comes in various ways,
surfaces in your awareness,
<u>as you try yourself,</u>
<u>your actual self,</u>
<u>your identity, on for size.</u>

KEYS TO ACCESSING THE BEYOND

Our developing our awareness
<u>of basic matrix shifting concepts</u>
(such as the KEYS offered in this book)
facilitates our matrix shifting capability,
reminds us of what
we already know deep inside our<u>selves</u>.

I have offered this book to help
revive, activate,
the higher level migration,
TRANSmigrational elevation,
instincts of our species.

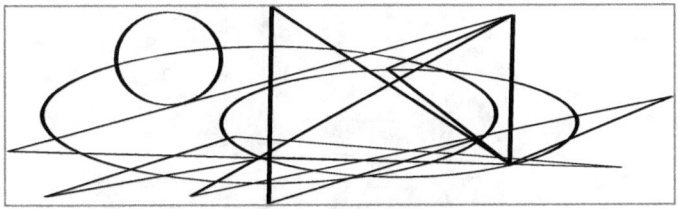

Basic matrix shifting involves the
shifting of our awareness, essentially…
moving our focus
from one place or <u>locus</u> to another,
focusing our attention on
key points or places,
whether or not these are physical.

In this sense, we are often
shifting our awareness, our focus,
even in our daily lives in this
physical plane.

Expansion, Elevation, Transmigration:
Survival Here And Beyond: Practices And Concepts

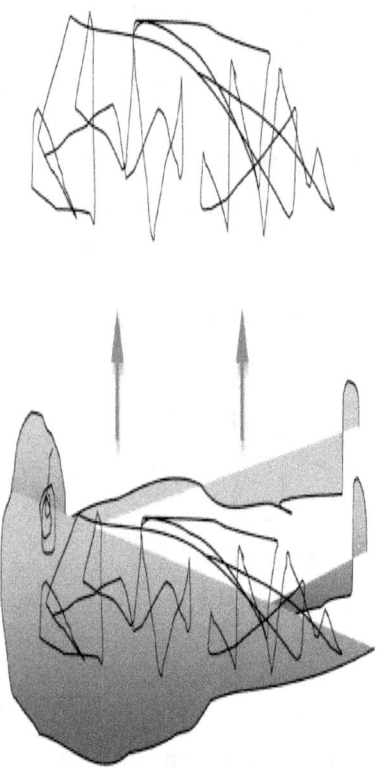

ELEVATIONAL

KEYS TO ACCESSING THE BEYOND

CHAPTER 12
Continuously Elevate Along The Dimensional Continuum

KEY #12
BE ALWAYS
MATRIX SHIFTING, ELEVATING,
TRANSMIGRATING

αΩα

Expansion, Elevation, Transmigration:
Survival Here And Beyond: Practices And Concepts

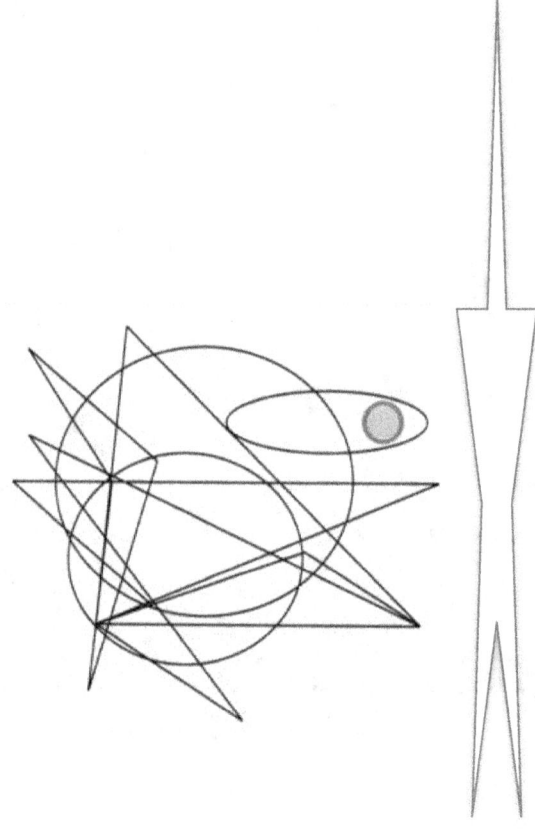

KEYS TO ACCESSING THE BEYOND

Weave

Weave this streaming light
Pulling strands
Filaments
Threads glistening

Intertwine these soft beams
On this loom of space
Warp and weft
Tapestry of energies

Vast iotas
Gleaming spindles
Sheer threads

Single fibers
Micro light
Nothing yet ever imagined

Expansion, Elevation, Transmigration:
Survival Here And Beyond: Practices And Concepts

KEYS TO ACCESSING THE BEYOND

TRANSMIGRATION/ELEVATION INSTINCT: KEY #12

MATRIX SHIFTING, ELEVATING, TRANSMIGRATING

1) Begin to consider, or *re*consider, your actual identity. Forming an understanding of your <u>non-physical identity</u> is an important step in learning transmigration. Know you are your matrix (of awareness, focus-energy, energy pathways). You, your matrix, is sometimes traveling in/with a physical biological body. You can move your matrix (SELF) with and without your physical body. Become aware of how you already shift your awareness and its focus in and out of physicality, without being entirely aware you are doing so.

2) Stay close to yourself, to who you are (which is your **matrix** as you hold it in your **focal point**), as you imagine or visualize yourself elevating. Be with yourself as your matrix, become more familiar with your matrix, its awareness, its energy pathways.

3) When you focus on pulling yourself to one focal point, *your* focal point, you will come to understand that you are pulling your own personal matrix to that focal point. No need to be concerned regarding whether such a complex matrix can fit into a focal point. 3-D size and 3-D dimension are not relevant here, as these are physical plane notions. Pull yourself to your focal point. Feel your pull, your cohesion, the energy you have there.

4) Scan your matrix for the energetic center of this matrix. If you do not find one, give that energy a center, a focal point, and concentrate the energy (which is your awareness itself) there. Use your imagination or visualization to form and find and be in the energetic center of your matrix, of your *self*. Know yourself as this.

5) Now find your focus already there, at this energetic center. Now move your focus, shift your focus. This shifts the energetic center of your matrix to move, shift, elevate, your matrix. You are shifting your focus to do this matrix shifting, elevating the energetic center of yourself, of your matrix. Move your focus to a few nearby OUT OF BODY locations. Then slowly return your matrix (yourself) to your physical body. Be aware of the shift from OUT OF BODY back to IN BODY sensation. Imagine your awareness stays focused, in its focal point, as you shift.

Expansion, Elevation, Transmigration:
Survival Here And Beyond: Practices And Concepts

KEYS TO ACCESSING THE BEYOND

About this
TRANSMIGRATION / ELEVATION INSTINCT: KEY #12
MATRIX SHIFTING, ELEVATING, TRANSMIGRATING

Know yourself better and better every day. Get to know your terms for everyday matters and for matters that may be far beyond your everyday reality.

Understand yourself by asking yourself questions regarding your own boundaries. Be sure you know how to protect yourself from being pulled without realizing it, from being pulled into actions and energies and patterns of others who you may not actually want to join.

KNOW YOURSELF, YOUR ACTUAL SELF
WHO CAN TRANSMIGRATE AND SURVIVE

You can get to better and better know yourself, you actual SELF, your essence, here in your daily life. This way, once you may perhaps be out there BEYOND, you can know who you have been and can continue to be.

This getting to know your self, your actual SELF, the essence of who you are, is about being familiar with your SELF as you survive BOTH HERE AND BEYOND.

KEY in surviving BEYOND is being ready to recognize your SELF out there BEYOND physicality, to know you still do exist. (Oh, here you are SELF: you have survived!)

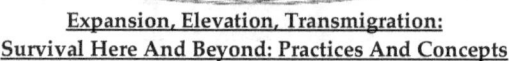

Expansion, Elevation, Transmigration:
Survival Here And Beyond: Practices And Concepts

Knowing who survives is KEY in surviving.

Pulling your SELF through a transition
involves
knowing <u>that</u> you <u>are</u> pulling through,
and
knowing <u>who</u> you are pulling through:
your
SELF.

SHIFT AWARENESS TO SHIFT SELF

Shift your focus and your center, and you are already shifting, elevating, migrating. We can <u>know</u> that this elevation is a <u>capacity of the consciousness,</u> a capability we are already applying and manifesting, as this is who and what the consciousness is and does. This is there for us to know, to SEE.

<u>Being a species of consciousness rather than simply a biological life form is not complicated, as this is what we already are. Hence, simply recognizing what and who we are is the first step in knowing these technologies of transmigration/elevation that I offer herein: TRANSMIGRATION TECHNOLOGY.</u>

Simply begin by being <u>aware of your awareness</u> itself. Begin the <u>matrix elevation process</u> by finding your focus, your FOCAL POINT, and elevating this focus, shifting this focus.

KEYS TO ACCESSING THE BEYOND

As I continue to explain on the following pages, the <u>transmigration/elevation technologies</u> I am offering herein begin with these:

matrix shifting (MS) first involves
focus (F) shifting (S) = (focus shifting, FS).

This **FS** is triggered at the center of your
focus pathways (FPaths)
where you can consciously
locate your SELF at your **focal point (FP).**

Shifting of the **energetic center of your matrix (EnCM)**
is key in shifting your entire matrix, your actual **SELF**.

Hence **center of "gravity" (COG)** shifting
is the shifting of your **focus-energy (FE)**,
and thus of your **focal point (FP)**
and
is also elemental in
**transmigrating/elevating your SELF –
elevating your personal matrix.**

**Expansion, Elevation, Transmigration:
Survival Here And Beyond: Practices And Concepts**

Outside the physical plane
we are more likely to think of
COGs simply as
centers (Cs),
centers of focus
(which are actually awareness centers).
...

I tend to discuss
COG shifting also as **C-shifting**.

F- and **C-shifting** are key
in elevating matrices.
(Elevating and shifting are
of course not linear,
only are herein referred to as
rather linear for simplicity.)

As individual Humans,
we can consciously
move our focus in and out
of our own physicality
more and more
as we learn the
basic matrix shift (MS) concepts,
these
basic transmigration/elevation technologies
I am defining for Readers in this book.

KEYS TO ACCESSING THE BEYOND

Once we learn to consciously come and go from <u>levels</u> of our own individual awareness, <u>levels</u> of our own consciousness, we are able to purposefully travel along the **(inter) dimensional continuum** (the DC/IDC), signified by the vertical arrows in many of the figures in this book (although the linear notion of "vertical" itself may not necessarily be active in many other dimensions).

Once we realize we are able to travel along this
DC (dimensional continuum), as its
IDC (interdimensional continuum),
we can see how truly, even naturally,
equipped we are to travel,
to shift, amend, expand our
our own individual "energy" pathways.
We can also see that we are already in the
process of doing this as part of daily life.

These pathways intersect, bundle, share energy,
forming our personal matrix.
In essence, who each of us is
is our personal matrix (PM).
This is where our matrix of SELF,
our consciousness,
IS.
This is who can survive.

Expansion, Elevation, Transmigration:
Survival Here And Beyond: Practices And Concepts

AND ON THE SPECIES LEVEL

Now let's return to the species level aspects of all this. Once we understand that we as individuals have this personal matrix (PM), we can begin to build upon this understanding to see that we as a species have a **species matrix** (SpM).

The species matrix is the essence of
who our species is.
This is where individual and species
focus and energy
pathways intersect, bundle,
interact to form our species matrix.

We can parallel to the personal matrix,
where the personal consciousness lives,
to see that this **species matrix**
is where
our **species consciousness**
is generated and lives.

We are, via our consciousness,
equipped to shift, amend, expand
upon the *collective energy pathways*
of our Human Species,
which is our
Species of Consciousness.

KEYS TO ACCESSING THE BEYOND

When a *critical mass* of individual members of our Human Species is aware of who it is, of what it can do for itself via its consciousness, it then can, via its consciousness:

consciously move, shift, its personal and species energetic patterning and essence, as well as its

species focus
(SpF)
and
species center of energetic gravity (SpCOG)
along the
(inter)dimensional continuum
(IDC).

———

Expansion, Elevation, Transmigration:
Survival Here And Beyond: Practices And Concepts

When the critical mass of the species focuses (in a **species focus, SpF**) on its **species center (species COG)...the SpCOG)**
which we can think of as its

center or *center of gravity*,
then together, in a synchronized manner,
energy and intent can be aligned
in conscious focus.

Once this *species capability* is understood
(or remembered) by the species,
the species is then
consciously able to activate its
interdimensional mobility.
Now the species
(members of the species who choose to)
can *consciously choose* to travel along the
DC and IDC
to shift, elevate their awareness-es, themselves.

Our species can then do this shifting,
can then do what I call a
species metaxis, a species elevation, a transmigrational
elevation.
We as a species can choose to do this
as we wish to, as we need to, as we have to—
including to amend patterns, to heal,
even to survive.

KEYS TO ACCESSING THE BEYOND

***

Note that individual species members may choose not to elevate with other members of the species, as <u>this is always their option</u>.

Moreover, elevation is AT WILL, and does not activate when forced.

***

Once we understand that it is within our species' capability to TRANSmigrate, to <u>shift-elevate-expand (SEE) as needed,</u> to shift its **awareness with its focus and energy pathways,**

> **our species can then consciously, at will, elevate, move its consciousness, its awareness, (to LEAP) in and out of its own (at least conceptual) physicality to:**

- look at the Earth niche situation from a new perspective;
- see "down" into physicality from beyond physicality;
- amend and then return the focus center (FC) to the biospheric Earth niche; and or,
- leave, elevate, shift out of, the Earth niche, whether only temporarily or permanently.

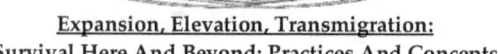

**Expansion, Elevation, Transmigration:
Survival Here And Beyond: Practices And Concepts**

**Again note that...
once consciously elevated out of the
physical plane Earth niche,
our conscious species can then consciously:**

- reach back down into its own 3-D physicality and work from beyond this physicality to repair, heal, amend, and or amplify, its own species life "down there" in 3-D; and or,
- move out of its own physicality in order to move elsewhere when the physical niche in which this portion of our species presently lives, (e.g., on Earth) is not safe in terms of species survival;
- or, for other reasons, expand itself back into interdimensional realms BEYOND where our species can live, has lived, and may choose to again, **live**.

**THIS IS ABOUT OUR
BUILDING ON THE "PERSON" MATRIX,
the PERSONAL MATRIX (PM).**

The personal matrix exists both separately and within the species matrix, does so concurrently. The notion of forming the species matrix (SpM) is quite simple once we understand what we already know on a deep level. We are an interdimensional species, a species of consciousness that is capable of tuning into its own species' interdimensionality,
its transmigrational elevation instinct.

KEYS TO ACCESSING THE BEYOND

As with the PM and IPM, we are also
moving our understanding toward the
notion of, consciousness of, the
SPECIES MATRIX (SpM) and
**INTERDIMENSIONAL
SPECIES MATRIX (ISpM)**.

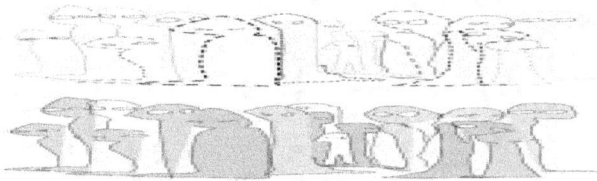

Yes, we frequently hear that ...
the whole is greater
than the sum of its parts.
We see this here as well.
We bring our individual
personal matrices (PMs)
together as a species,
connect these on an energetic basis,
and hence we are concurrently
the magnificent
species matrix (SpM).

Expansion, Elevation, Transmigration:
Survival Here And Beyond: Practices And Concepts

EXPANSIVE SPECIES MIGRATION

KEYS TO ACCESSING THE BEYOND

CONSIDER THE POSSIBILITY

Once you can recognize yourself, identify yourself as, not your biological body but your personal matrix, then you have a real mobility, your true mobility.

You then see, sense, this <u>mobility awareness</u> in yourself, and also where it has been activated in others. You feel this awareness around you, it starts to call you. Once you are alert to this <u>interdimensional survival awareness</u>, you will sense it in others who also are. No need to press for identification, this cannot be forced. <u>Your awareness will be aware of awareness-es who are aware. You will SEE each other, know each other.</u>

Simply wait to recognize and be recognized. The space of consciousness-es will be more and more clear to you. As you wait, always remember:

Your matrix is not itself restricted to the physical plane or to your physical body. This is your personal matrix, your actual individual identity. Each of us has the option of recognizing this within and about ourselves. We can never "require" that others see this or even wish to see this. Such awareness, like trans-migrational elevation itself, does not activate when forced.

However, it is important to be aware that suppression of this <u>elevation instinct awareness</u> may be taking place....

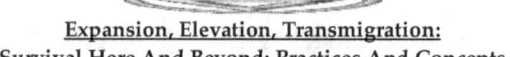

Expansion, Elevation, Transmigration:
Survival Here And Beyond: Practices And Concepts

Also consider the possibility that there may be forces or factors or intelligences who have designed us, programmed us, not to realize our true nature and our true mobility—and thus not to be able to apply this realization to our survival. This is a rather unusual concept, one we are likely not to consider from within the living laboratory where we may live.

I say "laboratory" here to suggest that perhaps we Humans on Earth are someone's lab rats, that we may be subjects in a grand (evolutionary or other) experiment virtually too large for us to see.*

Activating our <u>interdimensional survival awareness</u> will allow us to be aware of factors affecting us. As you do learn more about being a member of the Human Species of Consciousness, you will learn more about ...

clarifying and maintaining your personal matrix (PM), with its center (C), center of awareness (COA), center of gravity (COG), and its essential cohesion (COH).

Study the simple practices included throughout this book, the TRANSMIGRATION/ELEVATION INSTINCT KEYS. Be especially aware of the information on <u>cohesion (COH)</u> in *KEY #13* in this book (see next chapter).

Note:
This issue is detailed in the fifth and sixth volumes of this KEYS TO CONSCIOUSNESS AND SURVIVAL SERIES, titled OVERRIDING THE EXTINCTON SCENARIO, Part One and Part Two. See reading list at end of this present book.*

KEYS TO ACCESSING THE BEYOND

FREE OF LIMITING DEFINITION

However individual our experience of living is, we do have this greater and more encompassing experience of being part of this living species.

<u>Once we see how free we can be of limiting definitions of who we are, we can also see how expansive our existence is. We can also see (sense, feel, know) ourselves both as individuals and as members of our species.</u>

<u>Once you can more and more recognize yourself, identify yourself, not only as your individual matrix, but also as part of your species matrix, then you have this "higher" level matrix identity, which is that of your species.</u>

Too often, we live as individuals and forget that: we are part of a species; we breathe as a species; *we survive as a species.* This is likely quite obvious to all Readers, however we tend to overlook this profound reality as we live our daily lives.

Yet, our species is not only its physicality,

…just as individuals are not only their physicality.

Expansion, Elevation, Transmigration:
Survival Here And Beyond: Practices And Concepts

We can build upon the visualization of personal elevation to envision a species level elevation.

Once we
consciously understand…

- moving to and from the various levels (or dimensions)
via our own personal energy matrices, and,

- as I have earlier defined, the **personal metaxis** this
movement or shifting generates …

- then we can visualize this sort of moving together
(shifting, elevating)
to and from various levels
and dimensions
as a species.

This is basically a remembering
of what we already know,
of what our species already knows,
of what I call here the
species metaxis.

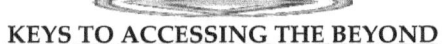
KEYS TO ACCESSING THE BEYOND

KNOW ABOUT SPECIES METAXIS...
META—AXIS....

This *species metaxis* takes place when the *species matrix elevates* out of the physical plane niche, moving along, through, within, the **inter***dimensional continuum and its matrix (IDC/IDM).*

The concept of *species metaxis* or *species transmigration/elevation* depicts a shifting of the species, the species which itself is the species matrix. And, as a species of consciousness, we are simply (re) learning what we already know:

TRANSMIGRATION.

When this shifting does expand beyond the physical plane to seemingly imagined or actual "non-material" realms, this is what I refer to herein as the

elevation, the transmigrational elevation.

This elevation may be temporary, or under certain conditions, where desired or needed for survival for example, even permanent.

Expansion, Elevation, Transmigration:
Survival Here And Beyond: Practices And Concepts

**THIS IS INDEED
ABOUT OUR
ACCESSING THE BEYOND**

When we as individuals think of leaving our physical bodies and of surviving as we do, we can think of moving our awareness out of the physical body or instrument that has been housing it.

There is so much we can consciously come to know (remember) about this process that can enhance this transmigration/elevation -- and thus our ability to hold our matrices together, *to survive,* **as long as we as individuals wish to.**

The species can also choose to move to and from, out and back into if it chooses, its physical body or instrument.

> The species can move as an energy matrix
> to and from its physicality.
>
> This SPECIES METAXIS
> can be the species moving its energetic center,
> its species focus,
> to and from the
> physical Earth Biosphere it inhabits.

KEYS TO ACCESSING THE BEYOND

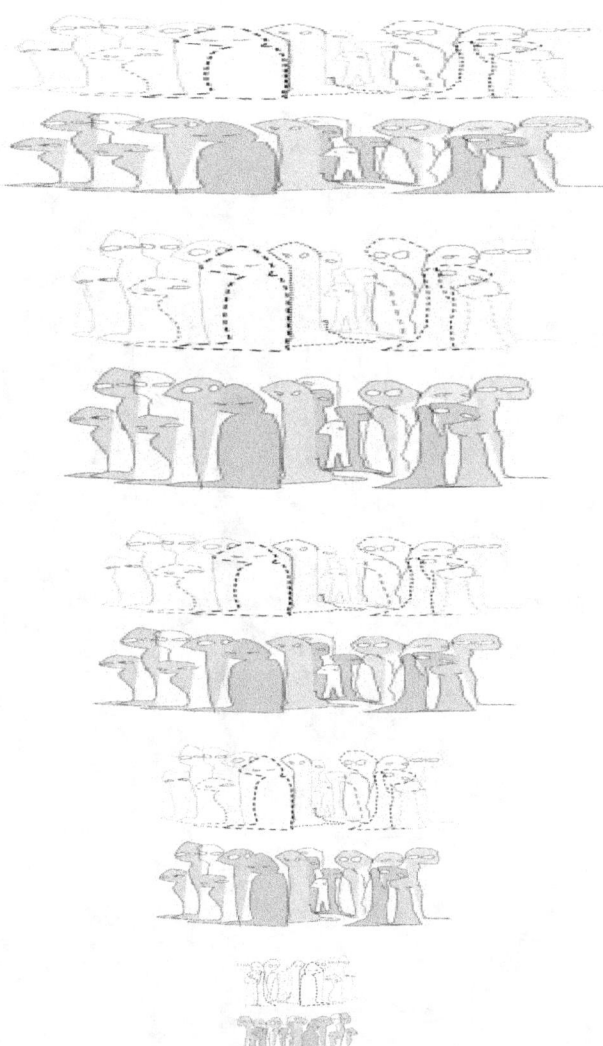

SPECIES METAXIS

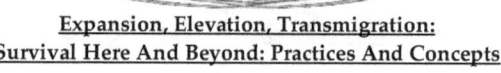

Expansion, Elevation, Transmigration:
Survival Here And Beyond: Practices And Concepts

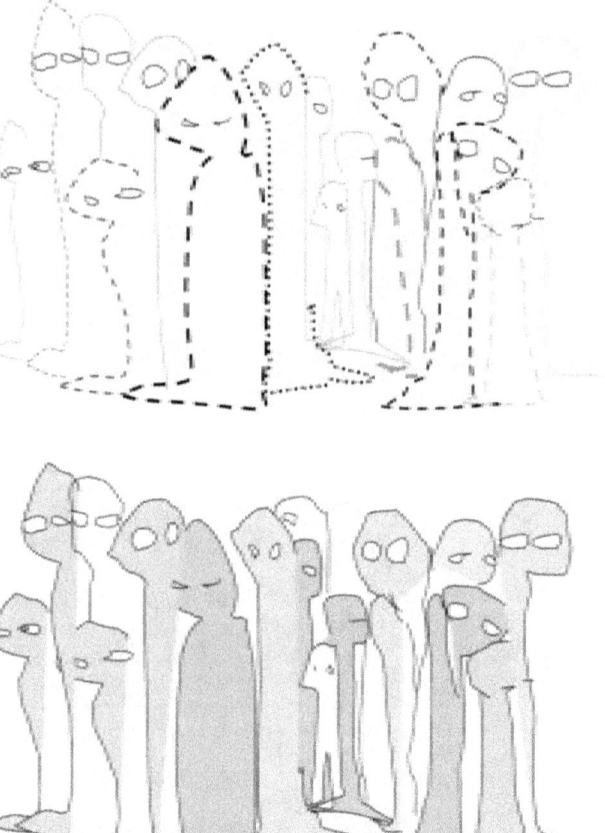

← ← DIMENSIONAL CONTINUUM → →

SPECIES METAXIS ALONG CONTINUUM:
Species Matrix Transmigration/Elevation
Elevating Out of Physical Plane Biosphere/Niche
Along the Dimensional Continuum

KEYS TO ACCESSING THE BEYOND

CHAPTER 13
Activate The Higher Level Instincts

KEY #13
INITIATE PRIMARY TRANSMIGRATIONAL EXPANSION AND ELEVATION PROCESSES

αΩα

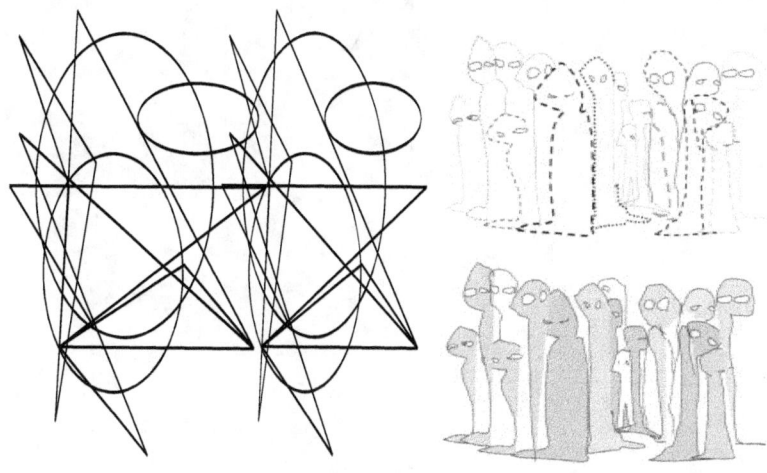

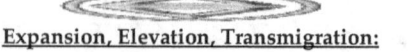
Expansion, Elevation, Transmigration:
Survival Here And Beyond: Practices And Concepts

KEYS TO ACCESSING THE BEYOND

Isolation Transforms To Connection

Again, the sense of isolation will pass.

Where at first there may be a sense of floating within an overwhelming immensity, thereafter there may be a sense of oneself (whatever that "self" is at this point) being of overwhelmingly miniscule smallness within that immensity. That sense may arrive with a vague "loneliness" in what at first may appear, seem, compute, to be a vast uninhabited cosmos....

If you find yourself in this sense, just be there. Stay present. Simply be, exist in that moment, regaining awareness, coalescing a conscious awareness, an awareness of this awareness....

Any sense of isolation soon morphs to, emerges into, a connection with the energy, the consciousness, even intelligence, of one's own as well as of other matrices out there ... morphs to a sense of living, being, fluctuating with the life of the energy collection, with the present presences, and with their and your intersections of energies and cohesions.

While at first nebulous, the case becomes more clear, and you grow distinctly truly aware of these presences in time and space and beyond time and space. You are there ... and here. Welcome home.

Expansion, Elevation, Transmigration:
Survival Here And Beyond: Practices And Concepts

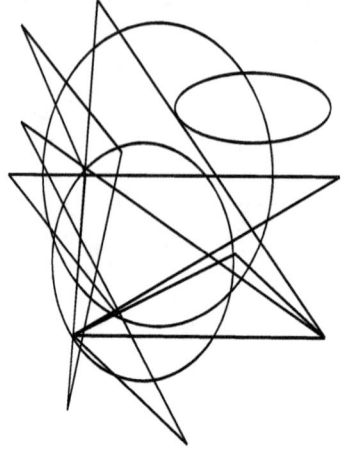

KEYS TO ACCESSING THE BEYOND

TRANSMIGRATION/ELEVATION INSTINCT: KEY #13

INITIATE PRIMARY TRANSMIGRATIONAL EXPANSION AND ELEVATION PROCESSES

1) Tune into the <u>awareness function</u> of your <u>consciousness</u>. Sense yourself heighten <u>your awareness of your own awareness itself</u>.

2) Select a <u>single point</u> within your physical (biological) body. Focus on this single point. Pull your <u>focus</u> (F) to this point. As you do, focus more intently there. This is your <u>focal point</u> (FP). Sense your FP having a sort of "<u>gravity</u>," a pull toward itself. Have your FP pull your <u>awareness</u>, its <u>focus</u> (F) and its <u>focus energy</u> (FE) more and more to this point.

3) Find the center of your FP. If you find no certain center, use your awareness to imagine or visualize there is one, a <u>center of awareness</u> (COA) there.

4) Feel the energy there at the center of your FP, the <u>center of its gravity</u> (COG). This becomes the <u>energetic center</u> (EC) of your FP.

5) <u>Scan yourself</u> to be sure you have pulled as much as you can of your awareness, focus, energy of your awareness and focus energy (FE), to the center of your focal point (FP). Feel the pull to this center, this COG of your FP. Now begin to feel the way this pull collects there and then holds together as your <u>cohesion</u> (COH), at this <u>center of cohesion</u> (CCOH). Be in this center of your FP and feel this <u>cohesion</u> (COH). At the <u>center of your cohesion</u> (CCOH), become still more aware of how you have centered, collected, your presence, your <u>SELF</u>, there. Become ever more aware of your<u>self</u> and your <u>cohesion</u> at this single point, in the energy of this point.

6) Still staying within your physical (biological) body, move your SELF just a little bit. Move as your FP, knowing as you do you are moving your COA, with its COG and CCOH: you are moving <u>who you are, your actual SELF</u>.

7) Now select another point within your physical (biological) body. Move your FP to this point, noticing how you do this, how this feels. Then return your FP with its COA, COG, and CCOH to the location of your original FP locus.

8) Now select a point a short distance "outside" your physical (biological) body. Before you move to this point, be certain your <u>awareness, focus, and focus-energy</u> is still collected at your FP as you will be moving your FP with its FE, COG, COA, and CCOH. This is your SELF. Now, <u>DEsomatize your focus</u>, moving your SELF as your FP to the point you have selected there outside your body. Feel this shift, this elevation out as you transmigrate. <u>Focus to maintain your cohesion</u> as you move, shift, out. Now reverse this move OUT OF BODY and move your FP with COA, COG, CCOH, back IN BODY. Note the <u>REsomatizing</u> sensations of this transmigrational elevation out, then back in.

Expansion, Elevation, Transmigration:
Survival Here And Beyond: Practices And Concepts

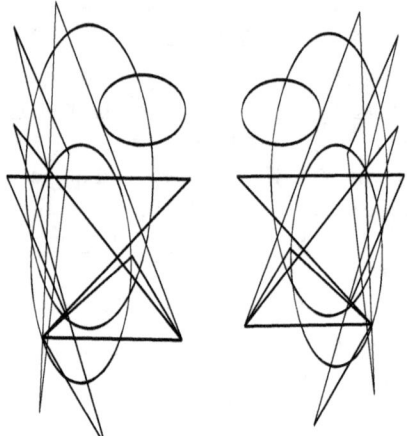

KEYS TO ACCESSING THE BEYOND

About this
TRANSMIGRATION / ELEVATION INSTINCT: KEY #13
*INITIATE PRIMARY TRANSMIGRATIONAL
EXPANSION AND ELEVATION PROCESSES*

✲✲✲

**CONSCIOUSNESS IS
TRANSMIGRATION/ELEVATION**

This book is presenting the notion of **conscious elevation and transmigration** in dealing with minor and major instances, events, impetus for, or needs for shifting from one state of awareness, one pattern of behavior or emotion, one reality, one organization of energy, one dimension of being, to another.

The discussion in this book seeks to **activate our higher level migration instinct, our TRANSmigration/elevation instinct, our species' transmigration intelligence.**

**Transmigration/elevation is an instinct,
also both a concept and a process.**
Once transmigration/elevation is underway,
this can be as instantaneous
as those transmigrating/elevating choose it to be.

In essence we are all elevating, transmigrating, on some level every day, every moment. We just do not tend to see our small and large shifts as transmigrations, elevations.
This book shares these concepts with
Readers and with Readers' consciousness-es
to trigger the knowings we have a right to,
as these are our essential knowings.

Expansion, Elevation, Transmigration:
Survival Here And Beyond: Practices And Concepts

**We are a species that is capable of applying its
consciousness to the changes, challenges, and needs
we face or may face,
applying our consciousness to live better, to feel better,
even to truly survive
where and when this is an issue.**

Readers are invited to
review these concepts listed
on these pages,
to open knowings within themselves

… and within the Human Species.

**After all, we carry this instinct within us.
And this instinct will surface once we
reveal to ourselves it is there,
once we read these words:**

TRIGGER ACTIVATION***
TRIGGER OUR INDIVIDUAL AND SPECIES
TRANSMIGRATION/ELEVATION INSTINCT
FOR USE AT WILL AS NEEDED.

NOTE: Some specific transmigration terms are being introduced on some pages of this and some of the following chapters. Readers are encouraged to read through the terminology paragraphs lightly, just to take in the general concepts – to gain a deeper sense of transmigration. Some Readers will want to learn these terms, and if so, see the glossary in the Appendices section of this book. Also see the in depth description and application of these terms in Volume 3 in this series, UNVEILING THE HIDDEN INSTINCT.

KEYS TO ACCESSING THE BEYOND

INTRODUCTION TO TRANSMIGRATION TECHNOLOGIES
TRANSMIGRATION/ELEVATION VIA MATRIX NETWORKING WITH FOCUS AND CENTER OF GRAVITY SHIFTING, LINKING, COHESION

(1) IDENTIFY MATRICES
Identify individual, group, species, biosphere/niche matrices (Ms) as networks, bundles, pathways of energies (POEs).

(2) SEE MATRIX INTERSECTIONS
See various networks in and among matrices cross-intersect to form cross-linked focus pathways (FPaths), pathways of energy (POEs), and cohesions (COHs) key in collective matrix shifting (ColMS).

(3) GENERATE, LINK, AND CO-SHIFT FOCI
Generate collective focus shifting (ColFS) triggered at the center of "gravity" (COG) of the cross-linked individual, species, and biosphere/niche focus pathways (FPaths) for shifting (ColFS at COG of FPs).

(4) CENTER, LINK, AND CO-SHIFT ENERGETIC CENTERS
Center collective cohesion (ColCOH) and energetic centers of matrices (EnCMs) key in shifting person, group, species, and or biosphere. Center of "gravity" (COG) and center of cohesion (CCOH) shifting are elemental in elevation of the collective matrix (ColM).

(5) MAINTAIN COHESION OF INTERDIMENSIONAL Fs, CFs, COGs, ColCOHs, AND COHs
Once out of physical plane, maintain focus (F) on collective foci (ColF) and centers of "gravity" (COGs) to maintain collective cohesion (ColCOH) of self, group, species, biosphere/niche matrices. Focus (F) on collective focus (ColF), center of gravity (COG), C-cohesion (ColCOH and COH) for co-shifting in meta-elevating meta-matrices (MEMMs), forming a matrix of matrices (MOM).

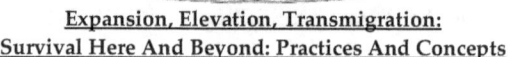
Expansion, Elevation, Transmigration:
Survival Here And Beyond: Practices And Concepts

The **technologies of transmigration/elevation** I introduce in this book suggest the **capability of Humanity to *shift its awareness*** in a profound way, to develop the capability to *migrate as a consciousness* if at some point survival pressures require us to rapidly "vacate" this biosphere niche in this physical plane.

WE CAN SHIFT INTO OUR OWN NICHE, WHICH IS THAT OF OUR CONSCIOUSNESS.

We as a species, or as members of a species or other group, can **(re) learn to shift our awareness, our focus, our center, in order to temporarily or permanently DEsomatize,** as needed for survival and other purposes such as healing, evolving, and expansion. We can SEE to LEAP. These shifts, expansions, movements from one focus (or locus or dimension) to another, are **transmigrational elevations,**
> in which the SEE, the shift-elevate-expansion
> facilitates the LEAP, the light-energy-action-process
> and vice versa.

The basic elements of these elevations are simple once (re) learned, as we carry these, they are instinctive.

****

Transmigrational elevation is facilitated by the *networking, linking, synching,* of personal, species, even biosphere awareness of the niche matrices among and within each other, depending upon what "level" of elevation is taking place: personal, group, species, groups of species, and or biosphere, etc.

When those seeking to shift do align and synch their awareness and its focus, connect their energetic centers of "gravity" (their C=centers), and then align their cohesion (COH), they can experience and activate their elevation and expansion across dimensions, realities, states of being.

KEYS TO ACCESSING THE BEYOND

CHAPTER 14
Be Elevating
The Biosphere
Matrix

KEY #14
UNDERSTAND COLLECTIVE
TRANSMIGRATION/ELEVATION

αΩα

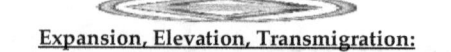
Expansion, Elevation, Transmigration:
Survival Here And Beyond: Practices And Concepts

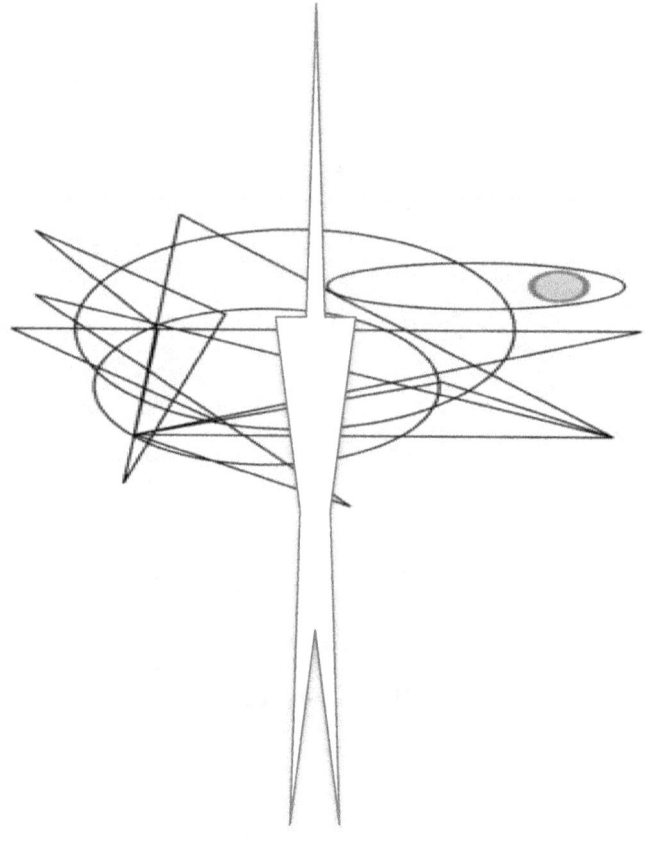

KEYS TO ACCESSING THE BEYOND

Never Ending Stream

By what amazing grace
have we arrived here
lost and found
ending and beginning
again.

The thread
the spirit of life
weaves on and on
as we intertwine
with all around
and all within
and all eternity.

Never ending stream
all things
we were
we are
and
we will be . . . .

Expansion, Elevation, Transmigration:
Survival Here And Beyond: Practices And Concepts

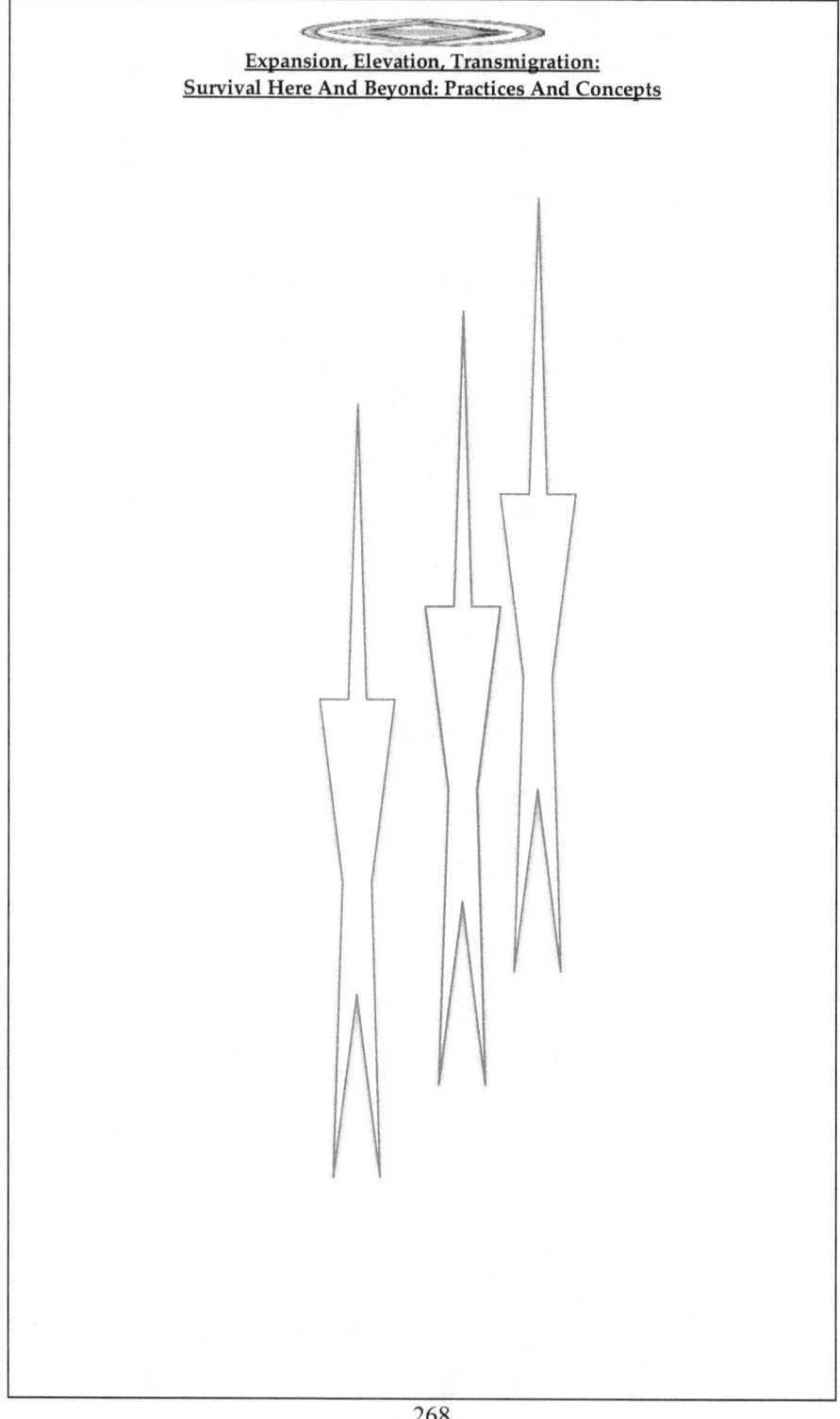

KEYS TO ACCESSING THE BEYOND

TRANSMIGRATION/ELEVATION INSTINCT: KEY #14

UNDERSTAND COLLECTIVE TRANSMIGRATION/ELEVATION

1) This is about *transmigrational elevation* of both individual and group awareness, consciousness. Just as do individuals, groups and even species, even groups of species, can envision parallel or even collective elevation of themselves.
2) As an individual life form, which is a member of your species of consciousness, you are also part of other life forms such as that of your species, groups of species, biosphere groups, and so forth. As a member of a <u>species of consciousness</u>, you will be more and more attuned to other life forms who are members of species of consciousness, who are also non-physical species although they are frequently traveling in physical biological bodies.
3) In your own elevation practice or actual process, as you pull your own energy matrix to your own focal point, and locate the center of energy in your matrix, others may be doing the same or similar in their matrices. Imagine how it will be to become aware of this. How will you sense this, how will this feel to you?
4) You can synchronize elevations at will, if you will this. The synchronization involves visualizing or imagining you are aware of others' elevation processes. Sensing the *elevation momentum*, which is generally at first quite subtle, can begin the synchronization. Again, only <u>at will</u> do you synchronize. If you choose not to, you will not. Synchronization cannot take place when being forced.
5) For now, begin to be quietly aware of sensations you may have, sensing other elevation awareness-es and their practices and processes. Be aware, stay aware of the <u>subtle energetic flows</u>.
6) When the time comes to know more, to join more, you will feel this, sense this, know of this option on a consciousness level.

Expansion, Elevation, Transmigration:
Survival Here And Beyond: Practices And Concepts

KEYS TO ACCESSING THE BEYOND

About this
TRANSMIGRATION / ELEVATION INSTINCT: KEY #14
UNDERSTAND COLLECTIVE TRANSMIGRATION/ELEVATION

STEPPING THIS THINKING UP TO BIOSPHERE LEVELS

We can build upon the conceptual process of **awareness elevation** (which itself is transmigrational elevation) as described on previous pages in terms of individual and species shifting. As shifting can take place along the (inter)dimensional continua and also throughout the (inter)dimensional matrices, we can envision other levels of shifting and of multiple shifting (including shifting of our single species and groups of species, even imagine shifting of biospheric levels). We can extend this transmigration concept to see that the idea of elevating the Human (and other) species' niche and biosphere matrix is a **HYPER-** or **META-METAXIS**.

Once we recognize the notions of…
- moving, shifting, to and from the various levels (or dimensions) of our species' matrix (species' energy body),
- and, the **species metaxis** this movement generates,

we can then think of, visualize, this same sort of moving of our still larger life form here on Earth, of our biosphere itself.

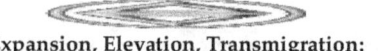

Expansion, Elevation, Transmigration:
Survival Here And Beyond: Practices And Concepts

We begin to realize, *to truly sense* on a fully conscious level, that we are not only a single animal but also a member of our species, and not only a single species, but also a component of our living biosphere (along with other species).

**In this sense, we are our biosphere,
this is the <u>level of living unit</u> we are.**

As individuals and as a species, we are living components of our biosphere. For we Earth Human individuals and for our Earth based Human species, the entire biosphere is our niche as much as our own particular physical niche within this biosphere is our niche.

It is the energy body of this biosphere/niche we perhaps can also shift, as we can shift ourselves (in personal metaxis) and our species (in species metaxis).

Remember, what we are shifting (elevating) is not the physical body, it is the consciousness, via its awareness, via its focus with its pathways of energy. As the shift is always of immaterial essences rather than physical bodies, we can SEE that it is consciousness that LEAPs.

We can envision shifting (elevating) our biosphere/niche as we grow more conscious of what this sort of transmigration, what I also call *metaxis*, is. Once we are considering the process of transmigration/elevation on not only an individual/personal level, or on a single species level, but on a group or even whole biosphere level, we are able to envision transmigrating our entire biosphere/niche matrix, shifting this whole biosphere/niche itself as an elevating life form.

KEYS TO ACCESSING THE BEYOND

This biosphere niche transmigration elevation is a **hyper-** or **meta-metaxis.** In this meta-metaxis, members of our biosphere can together shift awareness and its focus to and from levels of reality, dimensions. Our biosphere itself can shift along and throughout the interdimensional continua and matrices (IDC and IDM).

Perhaps someday, we Humans will seek to participate in, visualize, imagine, bring awareness to, this sort of conceptual…

<u>**biosphere shift,**</u>
**as a conscious species,
along with other species.**
****

We are more and more recognizing and seeing our
**INTERDIMENSIONAL SPECIES NICHES
AS REALMS OF OUR CONSCIOUSNESS.**

Once our species learns (or remembers how) to come and go from **levels of its species awareness**, it can (re) learn to have its biosphere/niche itself expand, travel, shift, along the **dimensional continuum (DC).**

Note again: None of this transmigration is physical per se. This is a shifting of the <u>focus of the awareness,</u> hence of the <u>focal point</u> (FP) where <u>the awareness, the self, is collected to facilitate this shift,</u> where the <u>pathways of energy (POE) are collected to the center of the matrix being shifted.</u>

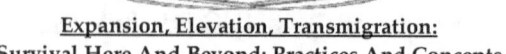

Expansion, Elevation, Transmigration:
Survival Here And Beyond: Practices And Concepts

On a deep level, we can see, **we can be consciously aware of**, how **truly equipped** our species is (and perhaps even the biosphere niche our species lives in and co-develops is) to **shift**, to relocate, amend, expand pathways of energy (POE).

Our species, as a biological life form on Earth, exists in this living evolving biosphere/niche, with this biosphere/niche consisting of this biosphere/niche's own massive energy matrix (EM). We have to now see the non-physical aspects of all this.*

When (a critical mass of) individual members of the species move its/their individual and combined personal and species matrices (linked and intersecting networks of personal and species foci, energetic centers of their gravities, etc.) in a synchronized manner, <u>the species can elevate itself.</u> Just as individuals can work together to shift their species, <u>multiple species</u> can work together to shift their biosphere, which is in essence also their biosphere/niche. In this sense, **species can work together to perform/<u>catalyze</u> the biosphere/niche metaxis of their entire living biosphere.**

Note: We can now see that what was once viewed as a "biofield" is indeed an **<u>energetic field</u>**, likely capable, **<u>or able to become capable</u>**, of existing with or without a physical body.*

KEYS TO ACCESSING THE BEYOND

However, it can be that some or many life forms we live with here on Earth (including many of our fellow Humans) may require the assistance and guidance of those who are fully aware/conscious of what is taking place. Assisting of other life forms in the metaxis process, *if and only if they clearly wish to join in*, may be needed. *We need not force this assistance on anyone. Elevation cannot be forced upon beings. Unwillingness does not elevate.*

HYPER OR META-METAXIS

Our species can help do this shifting for others among us (and for other co-existing life forms) who truly wish to join in. Ideally, those who wish to join in learn *or absorb by critical mass impetus* the concepts you are learning in this book so that they understand the basics of what is happening.

As there are no physical bodies or vehicles "moving," these shifts are conceptual products of the awareness, of the consciousness.

Expansion, Elevation, Transmigration:
Survival Here And Beyond: Practices And Concepts

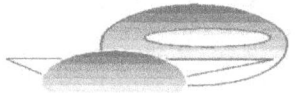

As always, once out,
survival and awareness
must remain central
as many beings, species, and even
biosphere/niches
may have "forgotten" about
surviving in the
nonphysical realm
after living in the physical realm
for some time.
(Or this knowledge may have been
evolved out of these life forms,
or suppressed in other ways.)

It may be that those of us
who understand these matters
will be called upon
to serve as teachers and guides
for those who come for such assistance.

KEYS TO ACCESSING THE BEYOND

← ← DIMENSIONAL CONTINUUM → →

HYPER OR META-METAXIS:
Species' Biosphere/Niche Matrix Transmigration Elevating Out of Physical Plane/Niche Along the Dimensional Continuum

Expansion, Elevation, Transmigration:
Survival Here And Beyond: Practices And Concepts

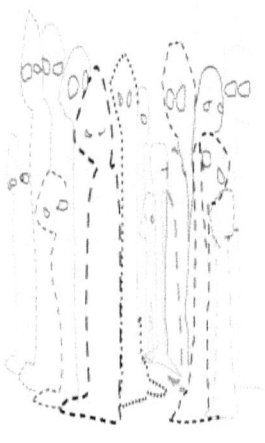

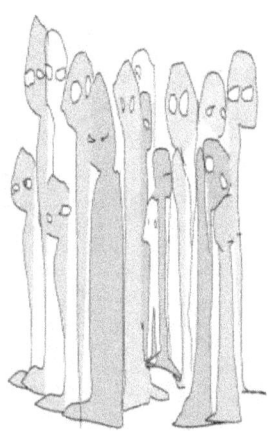

REACHING BEYOND

KEYS TO ACCESSING THE BEYOND

RETRIEVING THESE TRUTHS

We, as individuals, and as a species, as **a species of consciousness**, can recognize, develop, evolve, **adapt to (re)activate**, our interdimensional consciousness and capabilities. And the time for us to do this is **now**.

Again, we Humans do have the right and capacity to (re)gain, (re)assume), our rightful interdimensional awareness and intelligence. We carry this knowledge within us, thus this is a matter of our retrieving what is already ours from within ourselves where we have stored this knowledge.

Our interdimensional selves – interdimensional personal matrices – (our IPMs) are who we are, or are at least who we can be (again): highly mobile members of the Human Species of Consciousness.

Seeking to unveil this hidden transmigration instinct, I have developed the notion of the **transmigration/elevation technologies** I define in this book. I invite us to call upon ourselves to **retrieve the protected truths about ourselves** and our capacity to transmigrate for exploration, yes, and for healing and even survival.

The basic elevation processes, (the SEE to LEAP for METAXIS), involved in our shifting our activated awareness-es, ourselves and our species as a species of consciousness (shifting to new behaviors, new states of mind, new awareness-es, new realities, new habitats, new forms and formats) are in essence conceptual, energetic, instinctive, transmigration processes we already know. These are our instinctual understandings.

<u>Expansion, Elevation, Transmigration:</u>
<u>Survival Here And Beyond: Practices And Concepts</u>

We can consider this possibility....

When critical mass of awareness,
of <u>conscious consciousness,</u> is achieved,
this synchrony can even be achieved
between and among the
Tribe of Humanity
here on Earth and <u>beyond</u>.

This is about recognizing ourselves
as who we are:

<u>inter-dimensionally mobile beings,</u>
<u>consciousness-es,</u>
life forms who carry
this instinct, this capability,
deep within ourselves,
largely hidden below
our biological brain's programming,
below the biological coding blocking access
to this deeply stored knowledge and instinct --
<u>while this brain is currently directing, controlling,</u>
<u>our attention and perhaps even</u>
<u>limiting our survival options.</u>

For my theories regarding the mechanisms and science of control over us and our evolution, see reading list at end of this book, specifically Volumes 5 and 6 in this Series, which are the books titled,
OVERRIDING THE EXTINCTION SCENARIO, Part One
OVERRIDING THE EXTINCTION SCENARIO, Part Two.

KEYS TO ACCESSING THE BEYOND

TRANSMIGRATION ELEVATION: KEY ELEMENTS

- Synchronization of matrices can <u>fuel collective</u> (individual, group, species, and bio-niche) <u>elevations</u> along and throughout the dimensional continuum (DC and IDC) and dimensional matrix (DM and IDM) of the interdimensional reality where we do live, that we do have access to via our interdimensional awareness and its consciousness.

- These elevations involve the collective focus shifting (ColFS), collective matrix shifting (ColMS), and meta-elevating meta-matrix (MEMM) shifting.

- This powerful <u>collective synchronization</u> (ColSYN) <u>fueling, catapulting, energizing elevation to other realms of the dimensional continuum / dimensional matrix</u> (the IDC-IDM of the consciousness and its cosmos), involves the <u>alignment</u> (although nothing is really linear in this instance) via focus (F) and collective focus (ColF) <u>on focus pathways</u> (FPaths) which are energy streams as in pathways of energy (POEs).

- In this process, we can focus to *catalyze the elevation* of participating individual, group, species, and biosphere matrices, each of which is in itself a matrix of its own (M).

- Key in this elevation process (which is a catalyzation) are identification of and focus on the centers of "gravity" (COGs) of participating matrices via their centers of cohesion (CCOHs). This can facilitate the collective cohesion (ColCOH) bringing about the collective matrix shifting (ColMS) of group, species, and niche transmigration.

**Expansion, Elevation, Transmigration:
Survival Here And Beyond: Practices And Concepts**

LOOK FOR POWERFUL SYNCHRONY: FOCUS (F) AND SYNCHRONIZATION (SYN)

Indeed, this knowledge, this <u>transmigration/elevation instinct,</u> may have been stored so deeply to preserve it as we moved into the physicality of our biological Earth Human form. Our species of consciousness may have acted in the face of emerging evolutionary, genetic coding, or other forms of suppression of or blocks to our access to ourselves.

These blocks may have emerged via biological evolution, perhaps were naturally developed or otherwise implanted, or both.

We indeed can remember now that: <u>Inter-dimensional capabilities</u> can be (re) learned, (re) acquired, in steps and or in <u>collective shifts in awareness</u>. This collective move, <u>elevation via critical mass effect</u>, is a

powerful synchrony.

This book is about activating this extra and interdimensional capacity of our awareness functions within ourselves and our species. This is also about our understanding that this interdimensional awareness and mobility is quite natural and is our birthright.

This moving of a life form's <u>consciousness network</u> is the *matrix shifting* I am defining in this book. This matrix shifting is at once complex with many "moving" parts, interacting components, and at the same time, so very simple. We are indeed shifting, elevating, even transmigrating, in many ways at all times.

KEYS TO ACCESSING THE BEYOND

Yes, once the components are synchronized in focus, then the energetic centers can be and are coalesced, then the matrices are synchronized, then the shifting of the collective matrix can be instantaneous.

This instantaneous **collective shifting** can bring about the HYPER METAXIS I describe in the books in this KEYS TO CONSCIOUSNESS AND SURVIVAL SERIES. Of course this HYPER METAXIS can also be conducted in preliminary steps or focusing processes. Again note, transmigration technologies, including those of hyper-metaxis, can be acquired (retrieved) in steps or instantaneously.

ALL PARTICIPATION MUST BE VOLUNTARY OR THE ELEVATION IS STOPPED. SO DO NOT TRY TO COMPEL ELEVATION PARTICIPATION.

SYNCHRONIZE ONLY WITH THOSE WHO SIGNAL THEIR DESIRE TO JOIN.

Expansion, Elevation, Transmigration:
Survival Here And Beyond: Practices And Concepts

PRIMARY LEVELS TO SYNCHRONIZE FOR HYPER-METAXIS

There are three primary levels or energetic centers to be synchronized to generate the hyper metaxis....

**(1)
PERSONAL METAXIS:**
Individual Matrix Elevating Out of Physical Plane Species/Niche Along the (Inter) Dimensional Continuum

**(2)
SPECIES METAXIS:**
Species Matrix Elevating Out of Physical Plane Biosphere/Niche Along the (Inter) Dimensional Continuum

**(3)
HYPER METAXIS:**
Species' Biosphere/Niche Matrix Elevating Out of Physical Plane/Niche Along the (Inter) Dimensional Continuum

These conceptual levels can indeed build upon each other, beginning with the personal elevation or metaxis, then onto the species elevation or metaxis, then onto the biosphere/niche elevation or hyper metaxis. At each conceptual shift from one level to the next, full synchrony of intersecting awareness, foci, and energetic pathways can fuel the **successive metaxes** on "up" into the collective **hyper-metaxis** of the biosphere and even its biosphere niche.

KEYS TO ACCESSING THE BEYOND

SUCH A GRAND ELEVATION

Where such a grand elevation may sound to some a fantasy, or perhaps impossible, the understandings I introduce herein, these <u>transmigrational elevation technologies,</u> are personal, species, groups of species, and even biospheric **keys to interdimensional survival.**

These are <u>keys of consciousness,</u>
keys to CONSCIOUS awareness and CONSCIOUS survival.

These understandings can activate within our personal and species awareness-es our **advanced migration instincts and knowledge.**

Living beyond the expiration of our biological bodies (and their biological species bodies) is an option we have. Whether this is something we have always had guaranteed us, or have been able to do with or without particular rules and belief systems telling us they have the key, is an ongoing discussion, even in some circles a debate.

This book in no way tells Readers what position to take in this discussion. This book simply suggests that **whether or not our consciousness has always been able to exist independent of our biological body, our consciousness can choose to evolve itself to be able to exist temporarily or for good, independent of our biological body – if needed for survival: to shift focus, center, energy along the dimensional and interdimensional continua and matrices (IDC and IDM).**

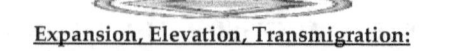

Expansion, Elevation, Transmigration:
Survival Here And Beyond: Practices And Concepts

WE CAN CHOOSE FOR OURSELVES

This book simply suggests that our consciousness can choose to recognize (to SEE) that our birthright includes our expansiveness, that our access to eternity or at least to our inter-dimensionality, OUR ACCESS TO THIS INSTINCT, is a choice we can consciously choose to consciously make.

And of course, this book simply suggests that we consider this option, that we consider this possibility, as we may want to and even perhaps need to know about this to survive.

As physicalized life forms, we tend to think that much of what we do not see (with our biological eyes) or cannot measure (with our biological brains and their sciences) does not exist or is inaccessible to us, and that there are thus mysteries we are not armed to address.

We have somehow become accommodated to this view of our limits, a view we are genetically coded to have and then biologically neurally wired to maintain. We have thus generally accepted without much question that our species is who it is programmed to believe it is, that what we as a species and as individuals think we are thinking is what we are thinking, freely and independently.

KEYS TO ACCESSING THE BEYOND

We fall right into line with the dictum of our biological programming, the coded-in biological <u>awareness restriction</u> upon us as individuals and as a species.

Any notion of our <u>consciously migrating</u>, consciously moving by means of our consciousness-es themselves, moving across various dimensions, in and out of other awareness-es, **<u>other niches of consciousness out there</u>**, is not generally accepted.

Rather, any interdimensional access or ideas are shorthanded, thus weakened of their potency. Then their access is denied to many others (by simply framing thus restricting these ideas as not relevant, or as only science fiction or fantasy, or as perhaps religious doctrine appealing to some people but not others, or perhaps as drug-induced "revelation" in the form of hallucination, dissociation, illusion).

This book presents the notion of shifting through dimensions via means of the Human Consciousness itself. Indeed, this is the nature of the Human Consciousness which is itself transmigrational. ...

As I have suggested in this book, we are actually a species of consciousness, *the* Species of Human Consciousness. And, therefore what we Humans do to interdimensionally migrate to and from places and spaces (transmigration) is far more a matter of moving our awareness-es, our consciousness-es, than a matter of moving our physical biological bodies.

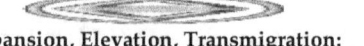

Expansion, Elevation, Transmigration:
Survival Here And Beyond: Practices And Concepts

I have found that the consciousness has the capacity to know far more about itself than the biological brain has allowed it to know. Indeed, our consciousness may even have been restricted in its knowing (in its awareness "functions") by our biological brain and genetic coding.

Our own Personal, Individual, Human Consciousness can, if it wishes to, conceive of itself as not being entirely tied to the biological brain. Once this possibility is recognized, or even merely imagined, the Personal Consciousness can explore the fuller capacities it may have available to itself, (capacities perhaps buried deep within, or even held there inaccessible or blocked from us), perhaps waiting to be (re)discovered, or finally now developed, evolved.

We can do this because indeed we do have the capacity to discover, even (re)design, new levels of the capabilities of our consciousness.

KEYS TO ACCESSING THE BEYOND

CHAPTER 15
Activate These Keys

KEY #15
CONDUCT EVER MORE CONSCIOUS EXPANSION, ELEVATION, TRANSMIGRATION

αΩα

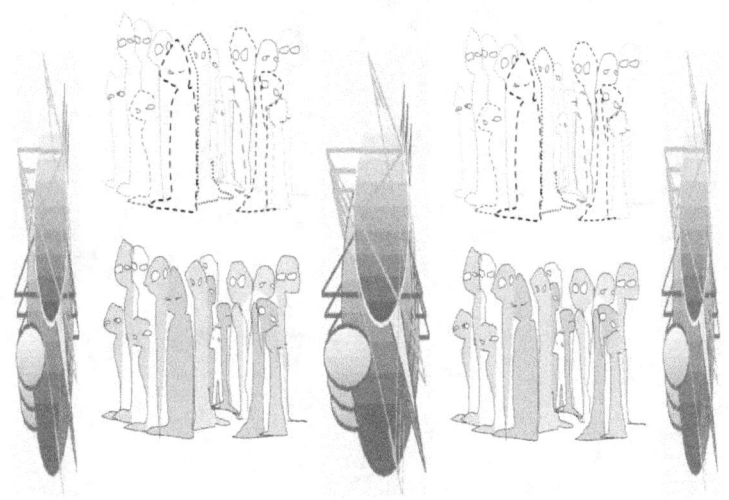

Expansion, Elevation, Transmigration:
Survival Here And Beyond: Practices And Concepts

KEYS TO ACCESSING THE BEYOND

The Door Is Open

The door to yourself is the
door to the cosmos.
The keys to travel are within you.
You, as an individual, and as a species,
carry the knowledge
to migrate to survive,
to transmigrate to truly survive,
to survive on an interdimensional level.

You can activate these keys.
We can activate these keys.
You, we, are these keys.
You can activate the keys
you carry within your consciousness.

Expansion, Elevation, Transmigration:
Survival Here And Beyond: Practices And Concepts

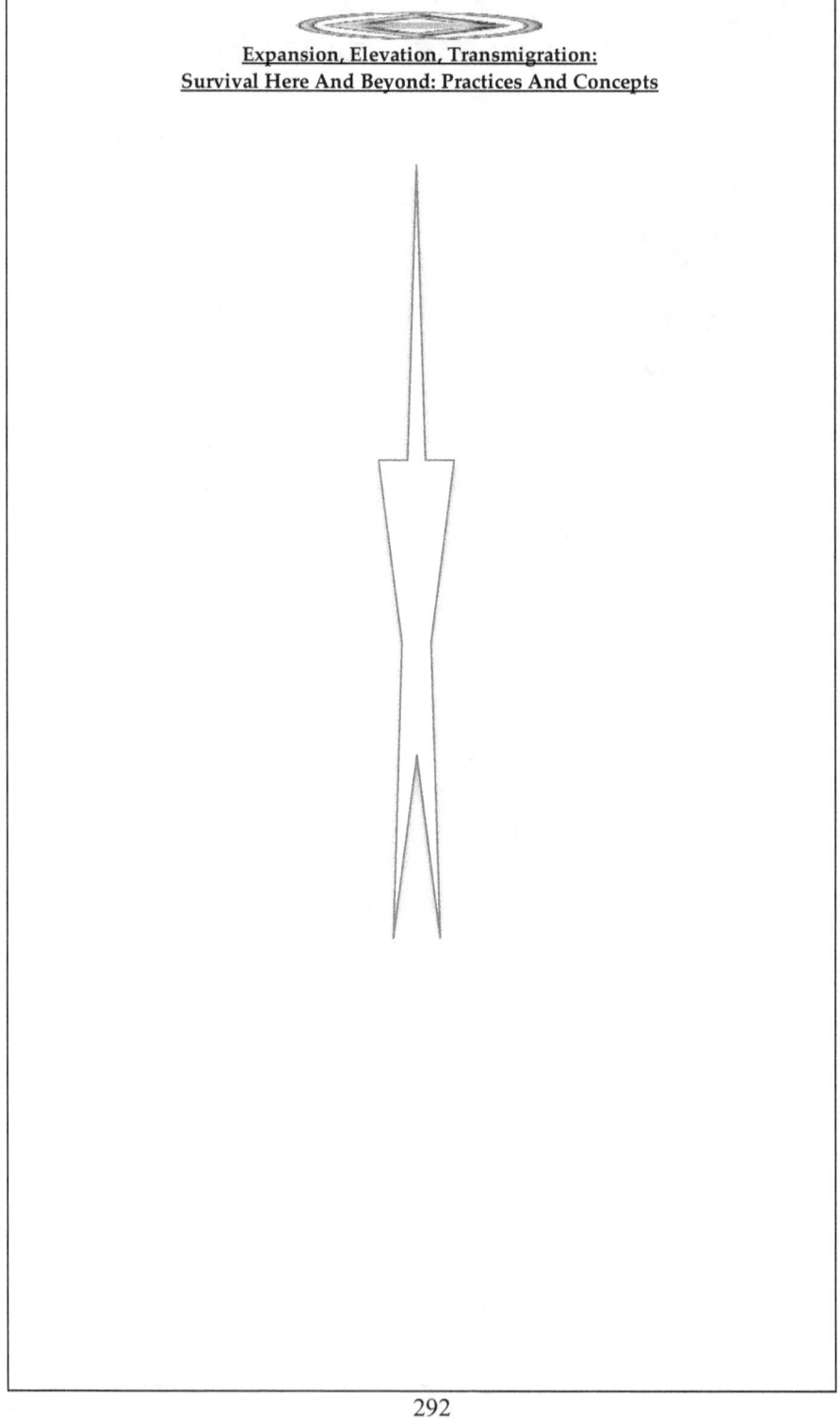

KEYS TO ACCESSING THE BEYOND

TRANSMIGRATION/ELEVATION INSTINCT: KEY #15
CONDUCT EVER MORE CONSCIOUS EXPANSION, ELEVATION, TRANSMIGRATION

1) As in the Key #13 and Key #14 Exercises, again tune into the <u>awareness function</u> of your <u>consciousness</u>. Now be ever more aware of your own awareness. Sense yourself further heightening <u>your awareness of your own awareness itself</u>.
2) Also, as in the Key #13 Exercise, again select a <u>single point</u> within your physical (biological) body. Focus on this single point. Pull your <u>focus</u> (F) to this point. As you do, focus more intently there. This is your <u>focal point</u> (FP). Sense your FP having a sort of "<u>gravity</u>," a pull toward itself. Have your FP pull your <u>awareness</u>, its <u>focus</u> (F) and its <u>focus energy</u> (FE) more and more to this point.
3) Now imagine that you are in a room full of other people doing the same thing – becoming ever more aware of their own awareness, then identifying a personal focal point (FP) for themselves, then pulling themselves to their focal points.
4) Feel the energy there at the center of your FP, the <u>center of its gravity</u> (COG). This becomes the <u>energetic center</u> (EC) of your FP. Imagine that others around you are doing the same. Now, imagine that you and the others around you choose to recognize each other's awareness-es and energetic focal points.
5) Imagine you ask those around you who wish to do so, to connect their focal points among and across the group. Imagine you feel the energy of the group become stronger as these energetic focal points are connected.
6) <u>Those who are choosing to are now moving their focal points together, beyond their physical biological bodies. Imagine or sense what it is like for the group to move their focal points to a shared point beyond their biological bodies.</u>
7) <u>As a group, select a locus, a location, for now just a short distance away – such as a ceiling or street light or other nearby place (perhaps a cloud in the sky overhead).</u> Sense your own and the others' <u>awareness, focus, and focus-energy</u> collecting there at your group's shared FP locus/location. Now, imagine that the members of your group have left their biological bodies -- have <u>DEsomatized for just a moment</u>, have moved their individual and group focus, their group FP, to the point you have selected out there outside their biological bodies. <u>Feel this shift, this elevation out as you all transmigrate. Focus to maintain your group cohesion as you move, shift, out. Hold for a while.</u>
8) Now reverse this move OUT OF BODY, and move your own FP back IN to your own biological BODY. Note the <u>REsomatizing</u> sensations following this group transmigrational elevation out, as you all move back in to physicality.

Expansion, Elevation, Transmigration:
Survival Here And Beyond: Practices And Concepts

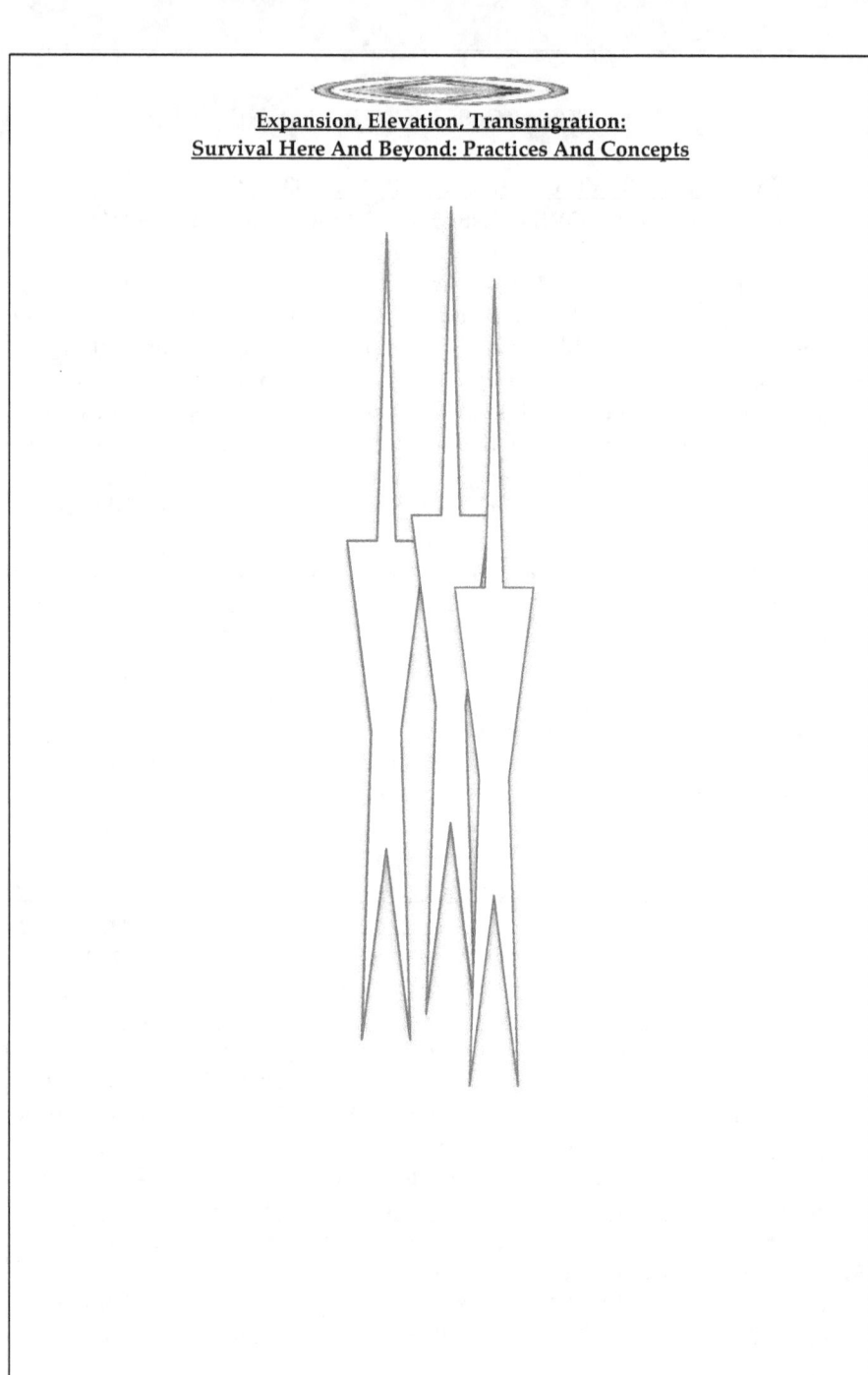

KEYS TO ACCESSING THE BEYOND

ABOUT THIS
TRANSMIGRATION / ELEVATION INSTINCT: KEY #15
CONDUCT EVER MORE CONSCIOUS
EXPANSION, ELEVATION,
TRANSMIGRATION

ON THE POWER OF THE IDEA
OF THE <u>BEYOND</u>
BEING THERE FOR US TO ACCESS

An **idea** is all it takes to open channels in the brain and mind, avenues into yourself/ourselves, to allow discovery by you of you, of us by us, of what secrets you/we carry about who we truly are. Feel your ideas surfacing, rising like truths, realizations within your awareness. Ideas can rise from deep within you/us, from places where these have been suppressed, or perhaps protected and saved for now when we can call ourselves to step forward, our truths to emerge.

Here, we experience <u>the idea</u> that we can form for ourselves <u>the idea of what we may find out there beyond our physical biological body</u>. The emphasis here is on the concept of the IDEA, because we want to open, further develop, and explore pathways in the brain and mind that can generate and develop this IDEA. This IDEA is a particular sensitivity, a subconsciously and even consciously exploring sort of awareness.

THINK ABOUT IT: **If you were an IDEA** –
would you know someone was thinking you?
If you were having an IDEA – when would you become
aware this IDEA was in your brain and mind?

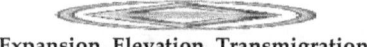

Expansion, Elevation, Transmigration:
Survival Here And Beyond: Practices And Concepts

When an idea is thought, many things take place in the biological brain.

Imagination functions as well as visualization and modeling and designing functions, among other functions, are triggered.

Think of an architect forming the IDEA of what she or he will be designing and drawing plans for. The IDEA must come first. Without the IDEA, nothing happens.

Then, from idea to vision to design to planning to actually building, there are a range of functions taking place in the brain, in the mind, then on paper, and then being built in 3-D physical reality. More and more these days, along the way, there are even 3-D models provided so that people can better visualize what the final outcome, the actual building, will look like.

Think of your SELF as your own personal architect. You are designing and building your own kingdom within and BEYOND. Indeed, when we are building our IDEA of a place REACHING BEYOND our physical plane reality, we are being this sort of architect.

Even what is taking place in the foundation is difficult to see, to visualize, as in essence this is taking place out of sight, on the micro-level, the cellular and even synaptic levels of the brain.

If we can open new pathways even in our biological brain while we are a living biological being, we may eventually be able to move along these pathways to expand into the next levels or dimensions of our SELF.

KEYS TO ACCESSING THE BEYOND

WE CAN REACH BEYOND

We can climb the stairs of our mansion, reach far past the foundation. We can climb up up up, and eventually step BEYOND physicality. Exploring these ideas builds the pathways, the stairs leading to our next steps.

In the meantime, exploring new pathways in our mind and brain brings us ever greater mental and even biological resources. These are resources we can know we have available to call upon. We sense we are more empowered, even in daily life. We can be ever more conscious of what we are doing as we are moving through the patterns and networks of patterns we live in and within.

When we learn to see and trace our path through our life, through the situations and networks and transitions we are living in and within, we can call upon this sensitization as needed, even much later---as we may find ourselves someday moving BEYOND our physical biological body, and find we can recall what we have learned here.

We can begin to see what is involved in moving through, even changing or releasing ourselves from, patterns and realities. We can see where there is energy that may be tied up, locked in, even trapped. This may be our own energy that we can release to use for ourselves and our survival as we move forward AND REACH BEYOND.

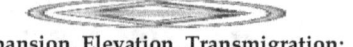

Expansion, Elevation, Transmigration:
Survival Here And Beyond: Practices And Concepts

BRINGING THE IDEA TO CONSCIOUS AWARENESS

Let's consider the possibility that ...
CONSCIOUS matrix shifting, CONSCIOUS transmigration/elevation, is natural once we understand what we have been <u>biologically wired not to know we know</u>.

Our personal and species consciousness-es can and must now consciously explore this notion of conscious matrix shifting, of transmigrational elevation.

As we do so, doors of possibility, even avenues of survival, we may at some time need to have (re) opened for ourselves, can be (re) recognized, (re) learned, (re) developed.

I believe that it is both the right and the responsibility of our Personal and Species Consciousness-es ...
<u>**to consciously know we know**</u>
<u>**and carry our transmigration/elevation**</u>
<u>**survival instincts and capabilities.**</u>

No matter how we Humans originated, no matter what beliefs we hold regarding our origin and purpose in this cosmos, I say we Human Beings can step in and consciously take control of the...
EVOLUTION AND SURVIVAL
of ourselves and our consciousness-es.

KEYS TO ACCESSING THE BEYOND

UNDERSTAND THIS AS METAPHOR

Understand this REACHING BEYOND, this ELEVATING, TRANSMIGRATING, as metaphor for PERSONAL AND SPECIES WIDE EXPANSION, EVEN SURVIVAL, **conscious survival**. The KEYS to and IDEAs/concepts regarding **consciousness expansion and shifting** I describe in this book can improve our understanding of ourselves, of our lives, of our realities, and of our survival options both here and BEYOND.

Each of us has an individual personal consciousness that we can share with our species consciousness (and vice versa). By seeking to discover, by thinking through, the **transmigration/elevation KEYS and concepts and their technologies** I define in this book, our individual consciousness-es are sharing these **think-throughs** with our Species Consciousness (and vice versa).

Expansion, Elevation, Transmigration:
Survival Here And Beyond: Practices And Concepts

We can reach past the <u>control</u> our biological brain has maintained over us, the control trapping us in a sort of
Dimensional IMmobility
and
Dimensional UNawareness.

We can spring free of, OVERRIDE, the ties and chains of our biological genetic coding. Sure, we can hold on to this coding to live in our physical Earth Human Bodies here on Earth, yet we must also know how to override this coding where needed for further survival purposes.

Note: Some Readers have written me and asked whether when I talk about overriding genetic coding, coding saying we can only survive in a physical biological body, I am talking about purposeful physical death to override.
<u>AGAIN I EMPHASIZE: No, I am not.</u>
<u>I am not talking about purposeful death or suicide as override.</u>
<u>This book is not about these things</u>.
The effectiveness of transmigration does not include this.

This book is about survival here in this physical plane, in the Human Bodies we have, and also beyond, learning what we need to know while we are here in the physical plane.

———

For my detail on and science of the brain's control over us, see reading list at end of this present book, specifically my theories presented in the books, OVERRIDING THE EXTINCTION SCENARIO, Part I and Part II (Volumes 5 and 6 in this KEYS TO CONSCIOUSNESS ANS SURVIVAL SERIES).

KEYS TO ACCESSING THE BEYOND

WE CAN AND MUST EXPAND OUR CAPABILITIES

I do hope we can retain our physical biological existences, even in the Earth niche where we live now. I do hope that the deterioration (or changing) of our biological Earth niche is not going to be so extreme that we die out of or must, to survive, entirely vacate this Earth niche.

This *conscious matrix shifting* I describe herein is valuable for physical biological Humans as well as for other forms of us, of our life form, we may someday wish to implement, activate, (perhaps even return to). Also note that I am suggesting that various (and perhaps essential) corrections of, refinement of, assistance to, our physical biological bodies and lives can be achieved by the **conscious matrix shifting** and these **transmigration technologies** that facilitate this shifting in and out, and even back into, this physical body and plane.

The matrix shifting I describe herein is an *expansion of our awareness* of who we are, an expansion of our capability to preserve, even protect, EVEN EVOLVE FOR OURSELVES, our Human Life Form.

This is an expansion of our species.

We can conduct this **expansion of our species**, those of us who wish to can, so that we are interdimensional awareness-es and interdimensional life forms rather than life forms restricted largely, even only, to being biological life forms living in this physical plane. This understanding is KEY in ACCESSING THE BEYOND.

Expansion, Elevation, Transmigration:
Survival Here And Beyond: Practices And Concepts

The highly conceptual expansion, shifting, transmigration of awareness/consciousness I present in this book is a valuable **expansion capability/concept** should we face survival pressure necessitating we vacate physicality and actually elevate, in part or in whole, beyond this Earth niche, temporarily or for good.

Again note: Readers who choose to believe our species is primarily or only physical and biological will perhaps find the KEYS and concepts that I have shared in this book a bit of a *leap* to accept as anything but fiction and fantasy. I understand this.

This leap itself, this leap in acceptance and understanding, is part of the evolutionary process this book seeks to help activate.

As I have explained, this concept about who we Humans really are says that our species is: actually a **species of consciousness**; is actually of the Life Force of the Human Consciousness Species; and is not simply a species of biological Human Bodies.

Where this concept may not be readily conceived of by some Readers, this is again alright. In fact, imagination is perhaps the best route for our brains (with their limited access to our full consciousness-es) to explore these ideas.

Go to imagination to share these ideas with yourself. Perhaps just explore all this and see where these ideas I write of herein take you. See what doors/pathways these KEYS TO ACCESSING THE BEYOND open for you.

KEYS TO ACCESSING THE BEYOND

THE POWER AND MOBILITY OF AWARENESS

Our assuming control of our own evolution may involve our **expanding (or reaching well beyond) our brain's capacity** to recognize, understand, and implement ideas that our biological brain has before now not been allowed to consciously know, or has only mildly addressed.

If focused concentration on particular thoughts, concepts, information, and or skills further develops the brain, further builds additional and or intensified neural and then energetic pathways, then other thinking, such as the **transmigration thinking** this book offers, may do this as well. We can be opening the mind/brain, spirit/soul, to the notion of the **power and mobility of the awareness**, and thus its ability to activate our ...

**transmigration/elevation
and shift-aware
survival consciousness.**

Expansion, Elevation, Transmigration:
Survival Here And Beyond: Practices And Concepts

KEYS TO ACCESSING THE BEYOND

CHAPTER 16
Know This Is Our Inter-Dimensional Survival Instinct

KEY #16
TAKE IN TRANSMIGRATION ELEVATION TECHNOLOGIES

αΩα

Expansion, Elevation, Transmigration:
Survival Here And Beyond: Practices And Concepts

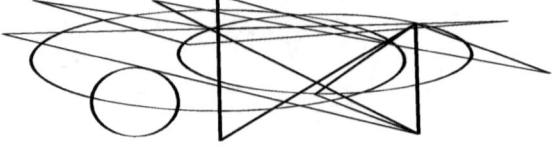

KEYS TO ACCESSING THE BEYOND

Moment Before Infinity

*Rivers of essences
Flowing like water made of nothing*

*Fine invisible strings
Washing into the flow*

*Creating the gloriously pure
Glisteningly sheer
Every day penultimate
Moment before infinity*

Expansion, Elevation, Transmigration:
Survival Here And Beyond: Practices And Concepts

KEYS TO ACCESSING THE BEYOND

TRANSMIGRATION / ELEVATION INSTINCT KEY #16
KNOW THE
TRANSMIGRATION TECHNOLOGIES

This KEY, KEY #16, is about knowing the <u>BASIC TECHNOLOGY OF TRANSMIGRATION/ELEVATION</u>, about understanding the sheer importance of this technology – and of the KEYS it brings to us. These are KEYS TO ACCESSING THE BEYOND, conceptual technologies of the mind and consciousness in the form of concepts, definitions, descriptions.

Here, let's start with some basic terms, and then, on the next pages, in the next section titled **<u>ABOUT THE TRANSMIGRATION/ELEVATION INSTINCT KEY #16: *KNOW THE TRANSMIGRATION TECHNOLOGIES*</u>**, several KEYS TO ACCESSING THE BEYOND are presented in the form of definitions and descriptions.

BASIC TECHNOLOGY OF
TRANSMIGRATION/ELEVATION

Note: In this book, I define and develop the terms, dimensional continuum (DC), and interdimensional continuum (IDC), also dimensional matrix (DM) and interdimensional matrix (IDM), for visualization, metaphor, and explanatory purposes.

<u>LEXICON OF TRANSMIGRATION</u>
I have designed these terms and concepts as part of this *lexicon of transmigration/elevation* that I have developed for this and other books, seminars, workshops, as well as for clinical, treatment, and research purposes.

Expansion, Elevation, Transmigration:
Survival Here And Beyond: Practices And Concepts

KEYS TO ACCESSING THE BEYOND

ABOUT THE
TRANSMIGRATION/ELEVATION INSTINCT KEY #16
KNOW THE
TRANSMIGRATION TECHNOLOGIES

The following terms, concepts, IDEAS, are KEYS TO ACCESSING THE BEYOND. Seeing the characteristics of the BEYOND we can access, and the pathways to access, begins by understanding some basics such as these:

INTER-DIMENSIONAL CONTINUUM
Our expansive consciousness is always moving along, throughout, what I am defining as the **dimensional continuum (DC)** and the **dimensional matrix (DM)**, that are in essence the **interdimensional continuum (IDC)** and the **interdimensional matrix (IDM)**. The **IDC/IDM** are one in the same, and extend beyond, are always moving to and from, physicality and other dimensions, densities. This is <u>not a complex process</u>. All that is required is to come into the knowing of what is involved in this awareness of, this *imaging* of, movement in and through the **DC/DM (IDC/IDM)**. This is a movement we are constantly engaged in, although not necessarily aware of. Yet, our consciousness already knows this movement, this ongoing transmigration/elevation process.

FOCUS and CENTER OF GRAVITY
We can move, can be moving back and forth, along and throughout the **interdimensional continuum and matrix (IDC/IDM),** by shifting our **focus (F)** and **center of gravity (COG).** →→

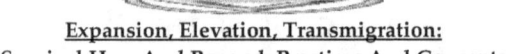

Expansion, Elevation, Transmigration:
Survival Here And Beyond: Practices And Concepts

CENTERS OF AWARENESS and ENERGY PATHWAYS

Once we learn to come and go from, shift our **centers of awareness (COA)** and their **focus (F)**, to travel along and throughout the **DC/DM** and the **IDC/IDM,** we are equipped to conceive of, be aware of, then in essence move, amend, expand, even rearrange, reconstitute, the imagined and actual **energy pathways (EPs)** of our and other participating matrices. We can SEE that from the DEphysicalized, DEsomatized perspective, managing and rewiring energy pathways in energy bodies is more readily conducted.

PERSONAL NETWORKS and FOCUS PATHWAYS

Our personal **networks of energy (NOEs)** are not evenly distributed and rather have **"centers,"** concentrations, of what I will call here, for the sake of this discussion, "gravity," thus **centers of gravity (COGs),** although these COGs are more like **densities of network pathway intersections**, what I describe here as **focus pathways (FPaths)** and related energies.

WE CARRY TRANSMIGRATION AWARENESS

We may not have yet fully (re)detected its presence and its full range of capabilities, however we already do carry this **transmigration/elevation <u>instinct</u>, awareness, deep within our consciousness.** We are able to <u>unveil to ourselves</u> this **essential survival awareness/instinct**, its awareness and its capabilities, to (re)claim these, as these are ours. We can begin this (re)claiming of our instinct by using ideas and imagination to explore the possible avenues of understanding, first working through creative processes and visualization. →→

KEYS TO ACCESSING THE BEYOND

ESSENTIAL SHIFT-ELEVATE-EXPAND CAPACITY

This interdimensional survival instinct is indeed our natural **shift-elevate-expand (expansion) (SEE)** capability: our understanding that we **can migrate** along the (inter) **dimensional continuum (DC and IDC),** migrate throughout the (inter) **dimensional matrix (DM and IDM), a migration, transmigration/elevation instinct, that may be essential to the survival of our species.** Yet our present time biological brains are wired to omit or block much of this from our knowing.

TRANSMIGRATION/ELEVATION TECHNOLOGIES

This book therefore introduces these TRANSMIGRATION/ELEVATION TECHNOLOGIES to help *activate* our interdimensional instincts, to fine tune their awareness facets, including *our own awareness of awareness itself,* which we may indeed need fully activated in coming times. By learning to fully shift our focus, we can shift, relocate, reformat, redistribute, our "energy," our *selves*. This can facilitate our moves to niches in other dimensions, places where we can choose to be, where we may need to be, where we can be safe if need be.

OUR MATRIX IS OUR ACTUAL IDENTITY

By moving our personal matrix (PM), we move what and who we actually are, the SELF. We move our identity, we move our consciousness, which is us. We move one increment to shift infinitely. We **shift the focus of our consciousness, our focus itself, which is who we are**. Our matrix naturally transmigrates.

Expansion, Elevation, Transmigration:
Survival Here And Beyond: Practices And Concepts

KEYS TO ACCESSING THE BEYOND

CHAPTER 17
This Is About Our Actual Survival In This Interdimensional Cosmos

KEY #17
EXPAND OUR SPECIES' CONSCIOUS SHIFT AWARENESS

αΩα

Expansion, Elevation, Transmigration:
Survival Here And Beyond: Practices And Concepts

KEYS TO ACCESSING THE BEYOND

New Focusing ...

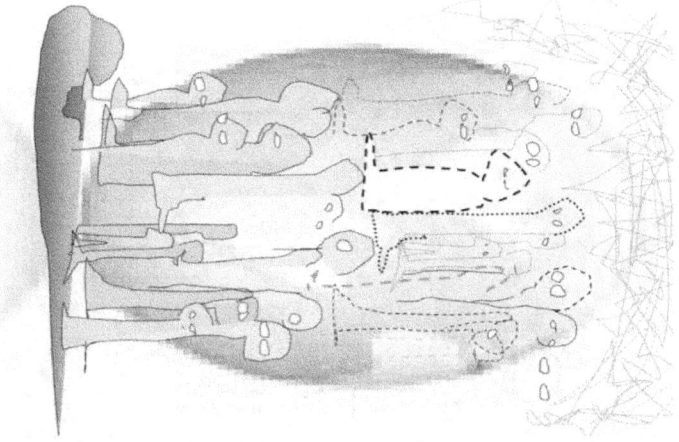

In an instantaneous knowing, we see with new eyes in a new seeing. Focusing the lens of our higher eye, we see what has been here all along – the BEYOND which is not entirely BEYOND as it is here now, always with us. We reach out and feel, sense, the presence of so much more here for us than we saw only a moment ago. Some higher lens is being refocused, as a cosmic microscope, adjusting to see the vast detailed opportunity waiting for us to notice. Yes, we return to the place from which we started, knowing this BEYOND now, knowing our KEY TO ACCESSING THE BEYOND is SEEING THIS BEYOND right here, right now, all around us.

Expansion, Elevation, Transmigration:
Survival Here And Beyond: Practices And Concepts

KEYS TO ACCESSING THE BEYOND

TRANSMIGRATION / ELEVATION INSTINCT: KEY #17
EXPAND OUR SPECIES' CONSCIOUS AWARENESS

INTRODUCTION TO KEY #17

Let's step back a moment to introduce this KEY #17....

This KEY, KEY #17, is about the expansion, the extension, the REACHING, of the actual SELF into realms BEYOND. This expansion, extension, reaching is in essence a state of mind (and of brain where we are living in a biological body with a biological brain).

We can develop our sensitivity and awareness of the IDEA of our non-physical non-biological self while we still live as a biological being. We can be becoming ever more aware now, of what may later be, our situations and options, such as when we are leaving our biological body in near death or even in actual death These are options we can develop for ourselves as we move BEYOND our biological body.

So this is about constructing, building for ourselves, developing, what I define (in other books in this KEYS TO CONSCIOUSNESS AND SURVIVAL SERIES) as **inter-dimensional competence**. The KEYS TO ACCESSING THE BEYOND presented in this book begin to build this competence in our biological brain and in our non-physical SELF. I say here "in our non-physical self," referring to this SELF that we can begin further developing by working through these KEYS. This is the SELF who can ACCESS THE BEYOND.

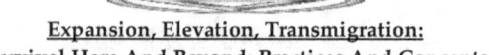

Expansion, Elevation, Transmigration: Survival Here And Beyond: Practices And Concepts

Building **inter-dimensional competence** involves **building a new construct for ourselves.** By "new construct" here, I am reaching beyond what is commonly considered to be a psychological construct that refers to states of mind, cognitions, attitudes, and emotions such as self-esteem and depression, that can be inferred by studying behaviors. I am also reaching beyond social constructs that refer to categories or things that are made real by convention or collective agreement, such as nationality or even time.

Now here, I am BUILDING AN INTER-DIMENSIONAL CONSTRUCT with these KEYS TO ACCESSING THE BEYOND that I am sharing in this book. I am saying here that as we further build our awareness and sensitivity to the experience of ever more consciously reaching BEYOND, we do ever more consciously reach BEYOND.

Therefore, this book and these KEYS TO ACCESSING THE BEYOND are KEYS to consciously ACCESSING THE BEYOND by CONSCIOUSLY expanding, elevating, transmigrating, SHIFTING our awareness, focus, presence, locus. (See again Key #4: Develop/Enhance AFPL=Awareness Focus Presence Locus.)

THIS IS
CONSCIOUS SHIFT CONSTRUCTION.

This *conscious shift construction* is indeed something we have a right to consider, to think about. This ACCESS is our right in living, in changing our lives, in healing our lives, <u>in healing our survival situations, in DYING AND SURVIVING, in ACCESSING THE BEYOND.</u>

KEYS TO ACCESSING THE BEYOND

THIS IS KEY #17

Key #17 is about understanding CONSCIOUS SHIFT CONSTRUCTION of INTER-DIMENSIONAL COMPETENCE.

Conscious shift construction offers opportunities to do one or more of the following:

- Move in and out of a state of mind or body at will, even if that state of mind or body is troubled, diseased, or deteriorating;

- Reach beyond, even leave, a state of mind or body in order to look back at that state of mind or body to see the patterns that occupy it;

- Work from outside that patterning to repair, rewire, redesign, rearrange the energy of, that patterning—after which the mind or body can be returned to, more free of troubled patterning;

- Consciously choose to either: return to the body that has been exited to address rewiring, healing, and or to navigate other in-life changes and transitions; OR instead, where elected, remain out of the biological body, and yes, move on from it, consciously move into the BEYOND;

- Move on when choosing to make the decision to move on, and do so consciously;

Expansion, Elevation, Transmigration:
Survival Here And Beyond: Practices And Concepts

- Understand that there are other phases of existence and consciousness, and learn the tools for travel within these dimensions of awareness.

- Preserve and enhance the consciousness no matter what the condition of the physical body(ies) it has traveled in;

- Move out of one vehicle into another or into a matrix itself — and survive;

- **Maintain *cohesion* of the personal matrix** as this moving or shifting (elevating) in space and time is taking place, as <u>your identity is yours to preserve</u> as long as you choose to.

KEYS TO ACCESSING THE BEYOND

**ABOUT THE
TRANSMIGRATION / ELEVATION INSTINCT: KEY #17**
*EXPAND OUR SPECIES'
CONSCIOUS AWARENESS*

**CONSCIOUS SHIFT CONSTRUCTION
IS A FORM OF MIGRATION,
IS TRANSMIGRATION.
THIS IS
OUR RIGHT
IN LIFE AND "DEATH"
AND IN HEALING,
TRANSITION,
AND SURVIVAL.**

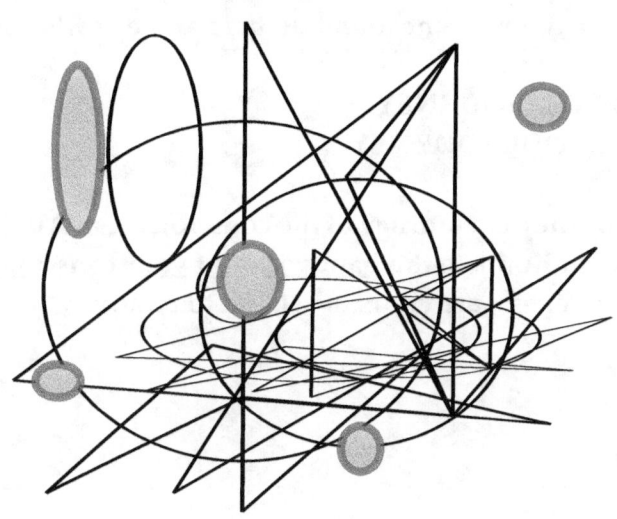

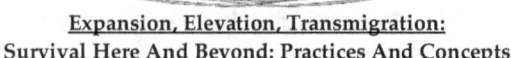

Expansion, Elevation, Transmigration:
Survival Here And Beyond: Practices And Concepts

YOU ARE THE CONSCIOUSNESS.

You are the consciousness which *constructs the shift* it chooses to undergo.

You are the consciousness which shifts.

<u>You are the shift itself.</u>

You are all pieces of this picture,
and you have a say in what
this picture looks like.

You are the gateway to yourself,
to your adventures in this life and its next steps,
to all that you will know and do here and elsewhere.

THIS IS THE JOURNEY.
THIS IS YOUR JOURNEY.

Every journey is a journey of the consciousness. All limits and removal of limits to the <u>bandwidth of your consciousness</u>, of your awareness, are yours to set and to remove.

KEYS TO ACCESSING THE BEYOND

YOUR CONSCIOUSNESS IS WORKING TOWARD
the iteration, exploration, purification, clarification, AND SURVIVAL of itself.

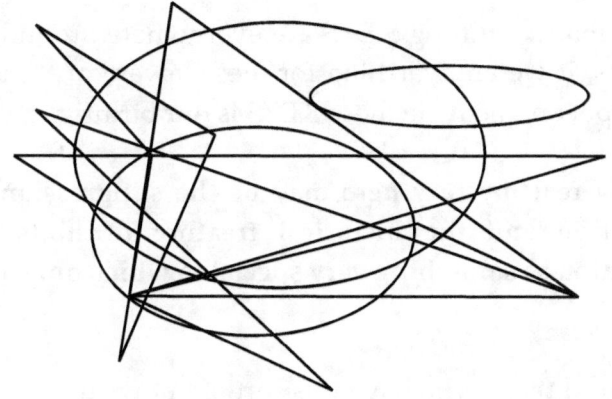

**Conscious shifting of our consciousness
can fuel
our species'
understanding and evolution –
the evolution of our
SURVIVAL ITSELF
BOTH HERE AND BEYOND.**

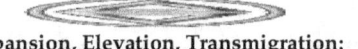

Expansion, Elevation, Transmigration:
Survival Here And Beyond: Practices And Concepts

The matrix shifting (elevation of our awareness and its focus) we may need to be able to consciously conduct (to effectively transit minor and major survival issues) are "mysteries" -- or have been described as mysteries by those who would control or even suppress this knowledge.

Yet, the matrix shifting KEYS are everywhere around us and within us, if we are watching for these, aware of these. Being able to spot and activate these KEYS is our birthright.

The only real mystery here may be the suppression of this information and the historical treating of hints of this information as something very special to which only a few are entitled.

Why would those who have this sort of knowledge try to keep it for themselves? To "protect" us or themselves, (*it*self)? Why would anyone with this knowledge seek to withhold it when it may be, or is, key to our survival, our species' survival?

KEYS TO ACCESSING THE BEYOND

EPILOGUE

Expansion, Elevation, Transmigration:
Survival Here And Beyond: Practices And Concepts

KEYS TO ACCESSING THE BEYOND

REALIZE WHO WE ARE.
WE ARE A
SPECIES OF CONSCIOUSNESS,
OF THE LIFE FORCE OF HUMANITY.

HUMANITY IS A
CONSCIOUS LIFE FORCE.

THIS LIFE FORCE DOES NOT DIE.
THE CONSCIOUSNESS CAN LIVE ON.

THE HUMAN CONSCIOUSNESS CAN
HAVE A SAY IN ITS EVOLUTION.

****

THE LIFE FORCE DOES NOT DIE.
YOU DO NOT DIE.
THE SPECIES DOES NOT DIE.

INTERDIMENSIONAL MOBILITY,
HENCE SURVIVAL,
IS OUR INSTINCT, OUR BIRTH RIGHT.

WE CAN LEARN WHAT
WE DO ALREADY KNOW,
TO TRANSMIGRATE
WHEN WE NEED TO DO SO, TO
SEE to LEAP for METAXIS.

Expansion, Elevation, Transmigration:
Survival Here And Beyond: Practices And Concepts

Freedom of Adapting To Our Rightful Interdimensional Mobility Awareness

KEYS TO ACCESSING THE BEYOND

WE CAN OVERCOME...
EVOLVED-IN LIMITATIONS

We, the Human Species living here in this physical Earth niche, can overcome whatever *limitations* we have acquired through evolution or have in some other way had implanted into our coding.

This will involve our consciously accessing the full scope of our keen Human Awareness and Human Intelligence.

We are far more than our biology, far more than our genetic coding, far more than what our brains program us to believe, to think, we are.

We can overcome the limitations upon our knowing set by our genetic coding and resulting brain wiring. Whatever evolved-in limitations we may have "been born with" or developed, or been programmed to have, we can grow conscious of and overcome.

**We can take conscious control
of our own evolution.**

**This is our right,
our birthright.
Our survival may depend on this.**

Expansion, Elevation, Transmigration:
Survival Here And Beyond: Practices And Concepts

Once we are conscious, once we access the full consciousness which is our birthright, which we have been biologically programmed not to access, we can generate ...

further degrees and capacities of consciousness, and its activated awareness,

for ourselves
and our species
and our biosphere.

Once we are
fully able to access the
full consciousness
that is who we truly are,
we are free
to survive
and to
access the beyond.

KEYS TO ACCESSING THE BEYOND

REACH BEYOND THESE PATTERNS

Leaving our biology-based patterns is difficult for us, as we have come to feel, are programmed by our brains to feel, we ARE these patterns. We tend to resist knowing on all levels that:

WE ARE NOT THESE PATTERNS, although our biological brains tell us to sense, to feel, that we are. We can thus <u>confuse our identities</u> with these lower level biological and emotional and social patterns, these webs we weave.

We can break free to see beyond our genetic and biological coding, the coding that plants and develops within us deep patternings our biological brains have generated for us to form and adhere to, to be controlled by. This breaking free, seeing beyond, <u>gives us access to the knowledge and instinct these patterns bury and suppress.</u>

These biological brain-generated patterns and the webs they weave within and around us tend to cloud (even block) our access to our actual identity, to own consciousness, to the instinct we carry deep inside – *to our ability to engage in our conscious shifting, our transmigrating, as naturally as do the many species who fly, swim, walk, to shift themselves, to migrate around the planet Earth.*

Expansion, Elevation, Transmigration:
Survival Here And Beyond: Practices And Concepts

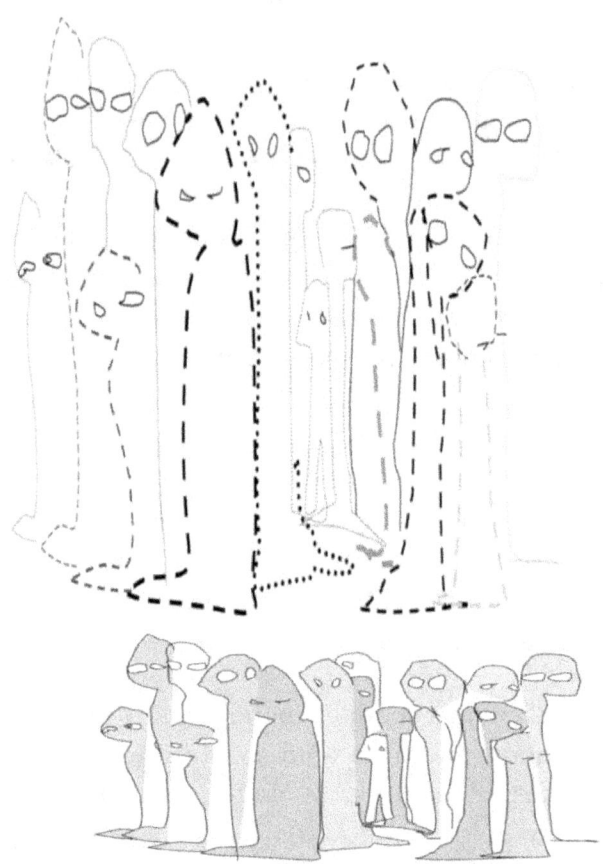

← ← DIMENSIONAL CONTINUUM → →

**Transmigration Drive
Under Survival Pressure In
Physical Earth Plane/Niche**

KEYS TO ACCESSING THE BEYOND

EPILOGUE NOTE

Your consciousness is seeking <u>to form a portal into itself</u>, into the realities it will detect and define. All limits and removal of limits to the bandwidth of your consciousness are yours to set and to remove.

We can pop out of the confining illusion. We can break out of the trap, the illusion we are programmed to believe is us, the 3-D reality we believe we live in and are defined by and tied to.

We can break out of this false trap, <u>release the energy stuck in the illusion imposed upon us</u> by this false trap. We can see how much energy is trapped in <u>the illusion constructed by our biological brain</u> that says we are only physical plane biological life forms who die when our biological bodies die. We are so much more than this. Knowing this is key to our surviving both here and BEYOND.

<u>**Expansion, Elevation, Transmigration:**</u>
<u>**Survival Here And Beyond: Practices And Concepts**</u>

We can harvest the energy released to use this energy to rise above AND EVOLVE.

This is our energy, your energy. You have cultivated this energy, and you can expand this energy into a new niche. You can use this energy to create a new niche, a new **ecosystem of the consciousness**.

There is no permission to be sought to reach this niche. This place is your birthright, this expansion is your option.

You can thus choose to participate in a healing of self, species, biosphere, even this Earth niche in all her dimensions: a personal, species, biosphere, and planetary healing.

KEYS TO ACCESSING THE BEYOND

AND NOW WE KNOW

We look around and see the astounding wonders of the amazing era we live in. At the same time, we see the great risks we face as our biosphere is undergoing increasing pressures and changes we hope and pray we can reverse or heal in time to survive them.

We are watching other species being threatened, even some becoming extinct. We cannot help but feel, on some level, the whispered threat of our own risk of personal and population, even species-wide, extinction.

We can still reverse this trend, however. We do know this.

We are now in a time when we want to reason with death, both as a concept and as a reality. Let's see that we can indeed survive, both here and BEYOND. It is time to fully embrace what this means. It is the actual SELF, the personal consciousness, that can survive.

Let's take the next step in our own evolution, and understand that the niches we can evolve into and for ourselves exist both here in the material plane and BEYOND. Once we master this awareness, we can survive both here and BEYOND.

Expansion, Elevation, Transmigration:
Survival Here And Beyond: Practices And Concepts

**we
are the
transmigration/elevation
itself**

KEYS TO ACCESSING THE BEYOND

THIS TRUTH ABOUT US IS OURS…

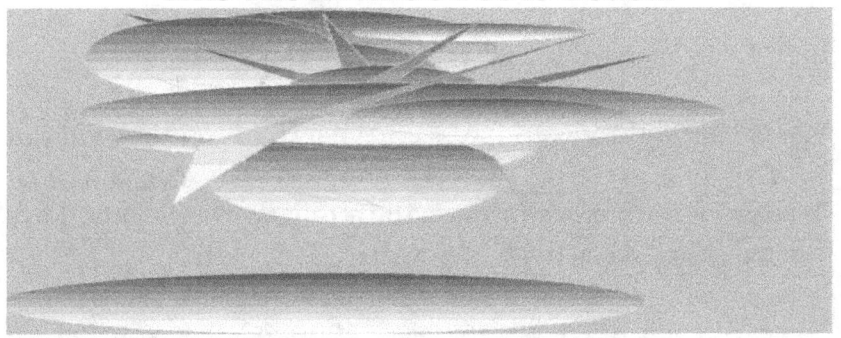

This is the truth about now.
This is the truth about the next phase of our evolution.
Survival in the physical plane is indeed possible,
healing of the planetary ecosystem is indeed possible,
however this requires expanding:
expanding into a new environmental niche,
**a new locus of the consciousness
to work from—**
and yes, to elevate to for good if this biological
physical plane niche we presently live in is
at some point no longer habitable for us.

This is the necessary truth about now.

Elevating, opening, and expanding,
beyond the gates of the physical plane,
can allow for the rewiring and healing required
by individuals, populations, species, even biological
biosphere niches.

Expansion, Elevation, Transmigration:
Survival Here And Beyond: Practices And Concepts

This elevating for the shift out—the SEE for this LEAP can be the KEY to survival in the face of a range of events.

We have a right to survive, we have a right to know we can survive, we have a right to the <u>keys to our survival</u>. Transmigration/elevation is within our awareness: the keys can be unlocked, activated, now.

Once you are offered the choice, informed that you have a choice to know or to not know, to think through transmigration/elevation or not to, the choice is yours.

The choice is yours—
and the right to choose is yours.

You can choose to recognize these
transmigration/elevation technologies
that can allow you, all of us,
to consciously shift
states of mind, realities, dimensions,
when and if needed for minor and major,
actual and conceptual,
shifts and changes,
elevations and transmigrations.

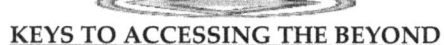

KEYS TO ACCESSING THE BEYOND

THE LIFE FORCE DOES NOT DIE. YOU DO NOT DIE. WE DO NOT DIE.

Expansion, Elevation, Transmigration:
Survival Here And Beyond: Practices And Concepts

← ← DIMENSIONAL CONTINUUM ↓ ↓ ↓

**Transmigration For Survival
By Species Of
Consciousness Of Humanity**

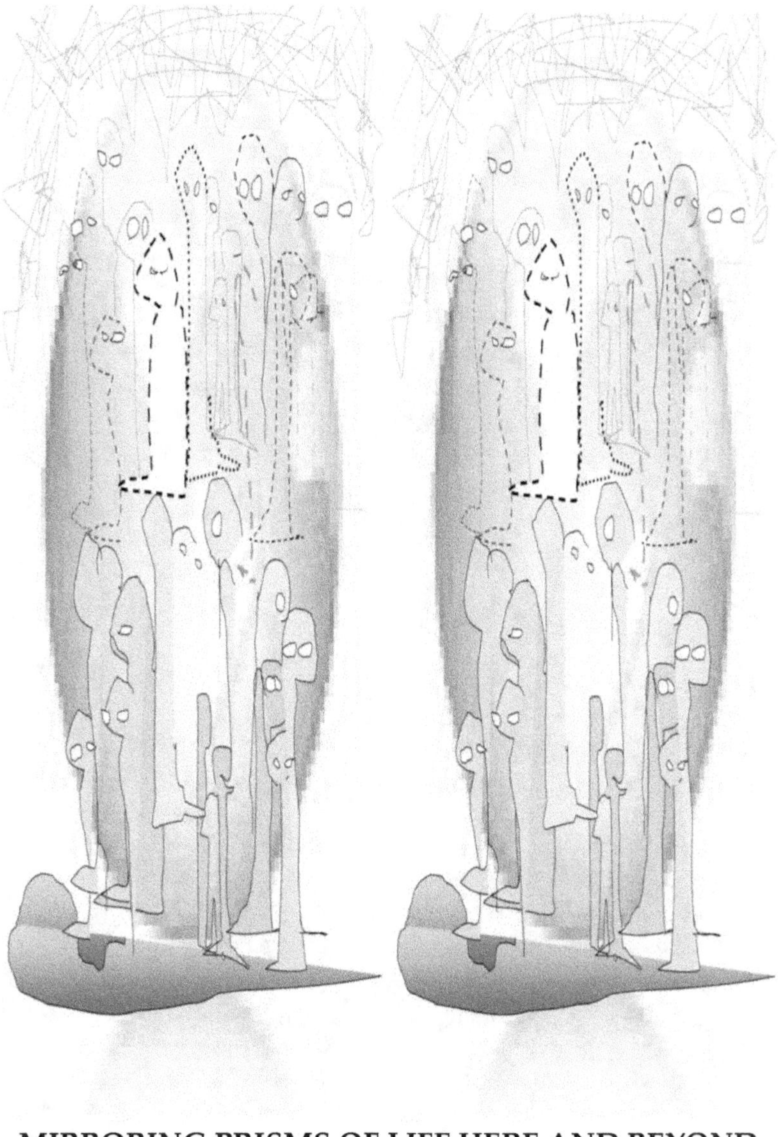

KEYS TO ACCESSING THE BEYOND

MIRRORING PRISMS OF LIFE HERE AND BEYOND

Expansion, Elevation, Transmigration:
Survival Here And Beyond: Practices And Concepts

KEYS TO ACCESSING THE BEYOND

All blessings
to you who know,
to you who do not know,
to you who know more,
to you who choose to come to know.

Expansion, Elevation, Transmigration:
Survival Here And Beyond: Practices And Concepts

Our consciousness
is entirely capable
of any transmigration
and elevation
we may wish to
or need to engage in.

That our consciousness
can itself be
a self-determining body,
a life form in itself,

is primary in
understanding,
evolving on a fast track,
activating
our
transmigration/elevation
awareness and
instinct
for our
interdimensional survival.

KEYS TO ACCESSING THE BEYOND

NOW, TO EXPLORE NEXT LEVELS

Further explore the possibilities of
your survival and journey both here and BEYOND.
What does this mean? What can this mean?
See ever more deeply into this consideration of survival:
What survival can be,
What practices can develop this survival,
What awareness-es we can expand upon,
And more....

Learn more about these
KEYS TO ACCESSING THE BEYOND
and these
KEYS TO CONSCIOUSNESS AND SURVIVAL
and the
HOW TO DIE AND SURVIVE TRAININGS such as:

TRANSITION NAVIGATION
LIFE-AFTER LIFE CONCEPTS
GENERATING THE IDEA OF THE BEYOND
SURVIVAL OF THE ACTUAL SELF

See the books and programs by

Dr. Angela Brownemiller at

Drangela.com and Amazon.com

Expansion, Elevation, Transmigration:
Survival Here And Beyond: Practices And Concepts

KEYS TO ACCESSING THE BEYOND

APPENDICES

Expansion, Elevation, Transmigration:
Survival Here And Beyond: Practices And Concepts

KEYS TO ACCESSING THE BEYOND

TRANSMIGRATION/ELEVATION ACRONYM LIST

The following acronym list has been defined and detailed in Volume 3 of this KEYS TO CONSCIOUSNESS AND SURVIVAL SERIES, titled UNVEILING THE HIDDEN INSTINCT. Several of these acronyms have been referred to in this present book, KEYS TO ACCESSING THE BEYOND -- and, in essence, these acronyms themselves are KEYS.

DIMENSION AND NICHE

DC = dimensional continuum
DCE = dimensional center
IDC = interdimensional continuum
DM = dimensional matrix
IDM = interdimensional matrix
DH = dimensional habitat
IDH = interdimensional habitat
EthN = Earth niche
IEthN = interdimensional Earth niche

FOCUS AND FOCUS SHIFTING

F = focus/focusing
S = shift/shifting
E = elevate/elevating
FS = focus shifting
FP = focal point
FC = focus center
FE = focus energy
SpF = species focus
SpFS = species focus shifting
ColF = collective focus/foci
ColFS = collective focus/foci shifting
C-shifting = CS = shifting of energy center

**Expansion, Elevation, Transmigration:
Survival Here And Beyond: Practices And Concepts**

PATHWAY
EP   = energy pathway
FPath = focus pathway
POE   = pathway of energy
EN   = energy network

COHESION
COH   = cohesion
ColCOH = collective cohesion
CCOH   = center of cohesion
ColCOH + CCOH   = C-cohesion

GRAVITY/CENTER
C   = center (center is of energy and/or of its energy's "gravity")
EC   = energetic center
COA   = center of awareness
COG   = center of "gravity"
COGS = center of "gravity" shifting
CS   = C-shifting (shifting of "gravity" of energy center)
SpCOG = species center of "gravity"
SpC   = species center of energy-gravity
SpCS   = species center shifting (species C-shifting)

MATRIX & MATRIX SHIFTING/ELEVATION (TRANSMIGRATION)
M   = matrix
PM   = personal matrix
IPM   = interdimensional personal matrix
SpM   = species matrix
ISpM   = interdimensional species matrix
BioM   = biosphere matrix
IBioM = interdimensional biosphere matrix

KEYS TO ACCESSING THE BEYOND

EthM = Earth niche matrix
IEthM = interdimensional Earth niche matrix
ColM = collective matrix
IColM = interdimensional collective matrix
EnM   = energy matrix
EnCM = energetic center of matrix
MOM = matrix of matrices
IMOM = interdimensional matrix of matrices
ELM   = elevating a matrix
EMx   = energy matriXing
EMc   = energy matriCing
MS   = matrix shifting
IMS   = interdimensional matrix shifting
MM   = meta matrix
MEMM = meta-elevating meta-matrix
NOE   = network of energy
ColMS = collective matrix shifting
SynEL = synergistic elevation
ColSYN = collective synchronization
SYN   = synchronization

SEE-LEAP PROCESSES AND THE REVERSE
Shift   = move awareness via focus across locations/dimensions
Elevate = "rise" out of a body, location/dimension (elevation is not "upward" per se)
Transmigrate = come and go from one state of existence, *awareness*, or "place" to another
Transmigration/Elevation = transmigrational elevation as shifting consciousness, via awareness through focus, out of physicality
DESomatize = move/shift energy matrix, focus, <u>out</u> of the physical (biological) body

Expansion, Elevation, Transmigration:
Survival Here And Beyond: Practices And Concepts

RESomatize = (again) move/shift energy matrix, focus, <u>into</u> the
       physical (biological) body
Somatize   = make physical, physicalize (biologize)

SEE   = <u>s</u>hift-<u>e</u>levate-<u>e</u>xpand/expansion
LEAP   = <u>l</u>ight-<u>e</u>nergy-<u>a</u>ction-<u>p</u>rocess
SELF Process   = <u>s</u>hift-<u>e</u>levate-<u>L</u>EAP the <u>F</u>OCUS

KEYS TO ACCESSING THE BEYOND

BOOKLIST AND RECOMMENDED READING

KEYS TO CONSCIOUSNESS AND SURVIVAL SERIES
by Dr. Angela Brownemiller

Volume 14
How to Die and Survive, Book Three:
Concepts For Living And Dying:

Volume 11
How to Die and Survive, Book Two:
Extending Our Interdimensional Awareness

Volume 10
Seeing Beyond Our Line of Sight:
Consciously Moving Through Life's Changes, Transitions, and Deaths

Volume 9
Navigating Life's Stuff – Dynamics of Personal Change, Book Two:
Keys to Consciously Moving Through Our Processes and Their Patterns

Volume 8
Navigating Life's Stuff – Dynamics of Personal Change, Book One:
Sensitizing to and Navigating Our Patterns and Their Processes

Volume 7
Keys To Accessing The Beyond:
Expansion, Elevation, Transmigration:
Survival Here and Beyond: Practices And Concepts

Expansion, Elevation, Transmigration:
Survival Here And Beyond: Practices And Concepts

Volume 6
Overriding the Extinction Scenario, Part <u>Two</u>:
Raising the Bar on the Evolution of the Human Species

Volume 5
Overriding the Extinction Scenario, Part <u>One:</u>
Detecting the Bar on the Evolution of the Human Species

Volume 4
How to Die and Survive:
Interdimensional Psychology, Consciousness,
and Survival: Concepts for Living and Dying

Volume 3
Unveiling the Hidden Instinct:
Understanding Our Interdimensional Survival Awareness

Volume 2:
Adventures in Change, Transition And Death:
Primer For Life's Minor And Major Challenges

Volume 1:
Keys to Self

KEYS TO ACCESSING THE BEYOND

BOOKLIST AND RECOMMENDED READING
Continued....

Ask Dr. Angela Series
Dr. Angela Brownemiller

—

The Bloodwin Code (Episode Books 1,2,3,4, and 5)
Dr. Angela Brownemiller

—

Transcending Addiction
Dr. Angela Brownemiller

—

Gestalting Addiction
Dr. Angela Brownemiller

—

Contact us for information on the special
Science Fiction Series
on these consciousness and survival topics.
Email:
DrAngelaBrownemiller@gmail.com

—

Note:
These books should be listed on Amazon.com and numerous other book distributor websites. If not finding these books on these sites and or in book stores, request these bookstores order these books, and or contact Amazon.com or Metaterra® Publications at Metaterra.com, or the author, Dr. Angela Brownemiller. Check also under last name, Browne-Miller. Thank you.

<u>Expansion, Elevation, Transmigration:
Survival Here And Beyond: Practices And Concepts</u>

ABOUT THE AUTHOR
Dr. Angela Brownemiller
Dr. Angela®

Dr. Angela Brownemiller, also known as Dr. Angela®, is an author, journalist, social thinker, clinician, psychotherapist, trainer, speaker, and creator of the ASK DR. ANGELA® Series of broadcasts, podcasts, books, audiobooks, Ebooks, and programs. The views of Angela Brownemiller are centered on the great potential of the Human mind, heart, and soul, and on the rights of all of us, who and whatever we are (or think we are). Dr. Angela Brownemiller views the Human consciousness as a wealth of opportunity for exploration, insight, knowledge—and survival.

**The works of Angela Brownemiller are brought to you by:
METATERRA® PUBLICATIONS**
(**and numerous other publishers**, see Amazon.com).
For copies of print books, audiobooks, and ebooks by this author,
see **Amazon.com** or **DrAngela.com**
DrAngelaBrownemiller@gmail.com
To take part in our events and workshops,
and or for personal consultations
in person or by telephone or online,
contact us at above emails and urls.

www.ingramcontent.com/pod-product-compliance
Lightning Source LLC
Chambersburg PA
CBHW050331230426
43663CB00010B/1817